Office 365 from Scratch

Peter Kalmström

OFFICE 365 FROM SCRATCH

Office 365 is Microsoft's brand name for a group of software and services hosted in the cloud. Using Office 365 is more convenient than maintaining your own server, and the security is high. You have less control with Office 365 than if you are using on-premises editions of Exchange, SharePoint and other important parts of Office 365, but many organizations find that this is a price worth paying.

Even if Office 365 is cloud based, several subscription plans also include desktop editions of common software like Word, Excel, PowerPoint and Outlook. Microsoft is constantly enhancing the platform with the explicit aim to make it more user friendly and easy to manage.

Office 365 from Scratch is primarily intended for administrators and other power users, but I hope the book also will be useful for others who want to learn about the possibilities given with their Office 365 accounts.

This book cannot be a full description of everything in Office 365. The topic is huge, and for more advanced users Microsoft has a lot of detailed information on their websites. Instead, I want *Office 365 from Scratch* to give an overview, so that you know what is available and which are the correct search terms for your continued exploration of Office 365.

Microsoft has developed Office 365 so that it is possible to get substantial benefit of the platform without coding experience, and none of my instructions and suggestions in *Office 365 from Scratch* requires knowledge of how to write code.

Office 365 is an ever changing platform which means that no book can ever be totally up to date with updates and new apps – not even the Microsoft websites manage that! Therefore, some things might be different and no longer work as described in this book. The steps will change, but if you understand why things are done the way they are, you will be able to figure out how to do things anyway.

Thus, I hope that the understanding you will acquire by studying *Office 365 from Scratch* will help you explore the platform far beyond the limits of this book!

Peter Kalmström

Contents

1 INTRODUCTION

In this introduction I have gathered some pointers and practical advice that you should be aware of while studying *Office 365 from Scratch*. I hope they will be useful to you!

An Office 365 subscription includes various apps and services. Most of these apps are also available as separate solutions, but in this book I will describe them as Office 365 content. All except the Office desktop apps run in the cloud and can be accessed in any browser and from any device.

Microsoft has made an effort to make Office 365 user friendly for touch screens and smart devices like mobile phones and tablets. Many controls in the latest user interface designs are easy to manage with a finger.

Nevertheless, to not complicate things I have used screenshots only from a Windows 10 computer in this book, and I have used the word "click" – not "tap". I am sure that readers with other devices can translate the information!

The Office 365 content varies with subscription level. I recommend the Enterprise E3 subscription, which includes all apps described in this book. Other subscription levels don't have all apps, but there is only a difference in quantity, not in quality. The apps work in the same way in all subscriptions where they are included. Therefore *Office 365 from Scratch* is useful for other subscription levels too.

Office 365 from Scratch starts with an introduction to the platform and information on how to set up and use it generally. Then I will go over to the three main parts that have been there from the beginning: Exchange, Office and SharePoint.

During the last years, Microsoft has added several new apps and services to Office 365, and I continue with a description of those. The most complicated are Flow, PowerApps and Power BI, with different usage areas but who all make connections between various platforms and programs inside and outside Office 365.

With the introduction of Office 365 Groups, Microsoft could add more apps, like Planner, StaffHub and Teams. Also the more mature Yammer is in the process of being connected to Office 365 Groups, and Office 365 Groups have become an increasingly important part of SharePoint and Exchange.

The demo URLs in *Office 365 from Scratch* refer to articles in the kalmstrom.com Tips section. Here you can watch video demonstrations on subjects that are similar to what I describe in the book. I hope these articles will give variation and bring a deeper understanding.

Let's begin! The first step is of course to set up Office 365 and add user accounts, and that is what we will do in the first chapter.

2   THE OFFICE 365 TENANT

Each organization that subscribe to Office 365 has its own password protected "room in the cloud". This "room" is called a tenant.

In this first chapter, you will learn how to set up and configure an Office 365 tenant for an organization and how to sign in to the new tenant and stay signed in. I also explain the different parts of the Office 365 Navigation bar. These parts are crucial to your continued understanding and use of Office 365, so I will take it in detail.

But first of all I will explain what the words "tenant" and "app" mean in the Office 365 context.

2.1   THE TENANT NAME

When you start an Office 365 trial, your organization is assigned a tenant. You can keep the same tenant and all the work you have done, if you decide to go from a trial to a paid subscription.

The data you add to the tenant is stored in Microsoft's servers, but your organization owns and controls the data. Microsoft does not use your data for anything else than providing you with the services that you have subscribed to.

When you set up your Office 365 trial, you need to specify a name for the tenant, and it should have the form NAME.onmicrosoft.com. The tenant name cannot be changed after you have started your Office 365 trial, and it must be unique.

2.2   APPS

Users can reach the Office 365 apps from the App Launcher to the left on the top navigation of all Office 365 apps and from office.com. When you click on an app tile, you will be directed to the online home page for that app.

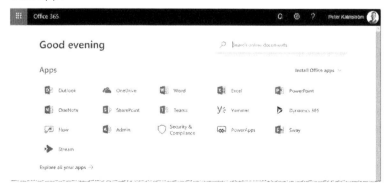

Each user will only see the apps he or she has permission to use. This means, for example, that only Office 365 administrators can see the Admin tile, shown at the bottom of the second row of apps in the image above.

Office 365 administrators can reach the app settings by clicking on the Admin tile. They are then directed to the Office 365 Admin center, and from there they can also reach the Exchange Admin center, the SharePoint Admin center and several other Admin centers.

2.3 SET UP AN OFFICE 365 TRIAL

Office 365 has several different subscription plans, but I recommend the Office 365 Enterprise E3. It contains some of my favorite features, like unlimited mailbox archiving in Exchange and unlimited file storage on OneDrive for Business. It also includes several useful apps such as Teams and Flow. Finally it gives you access to some of my favorite SharePoint web parts, like Excel Web Access and Content Search.The setup steps below refer to the Enterprise E3 plan, but the process is similar for other plans.

Office 365 is a web-based platform, so you need to start in a web browser.

1. Type the web address office.com in the address bar.

2. On the Office Online page, click on 'Products' and select 'Enterprise' from the dropdown.

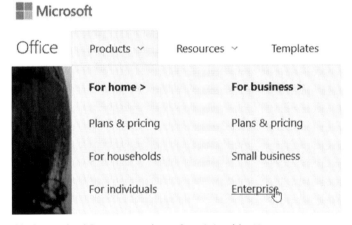

3. Click on the 'Compare plans & pricing' button.

4. Click on 'Learn more' under the 'Office 365 Enterprise E3' option.

5. Click on 'Free trial'.

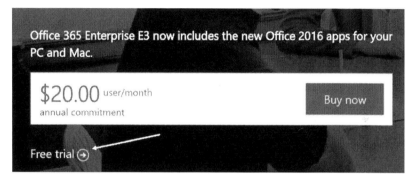

6. Select country and fill out your name, business email address, phone number and company name.

7. Select how many employees your company has. This does not affect what features you will have access to, as that was decided when you selected your subscription plan.

8. Click on 'Just one more step'.

9. Enter a user name and a tenant name (= "Yourcompany"). Note that the tenant name cannot be changed later. You can create new users, but they will all have the tenant name you decide on here – unless you create another Office 365 account with a new tenant name, of course.

Create your user ID

You need a user ID and password to sign in to your account.

10. Enter a password.

11. Check or uncheck boxes to decide if and how you want to be contacted by Microsoft.

12. Click on 'Create my account'.

13. To prove that you are not a robot, you need to give a telephone number for a call or text message. Click on 'Text me/Call me'.

14. Enter the verification code and click on 'Next'.

Now the trial account will be created. It may take 15 minutes before all is set up, but some parts of Office 365 can usually be reached as soon as you see your log in details and the text 'You're ready to go' on the screen. Click on that text to continue.

Even if all services are not set up yet, you can now start adding users to the new Office 365 tenant or install the Office 2016 desktop apps; *refer to* chapters 3 and 4.

Now you can use Office 365 for free and try it as a Global Administrator. When the evaluation period is finished, you need to subscribe to Office 365 to continue using the platform.

Demo:

https://www.kalmstrom.com/Tips/Office-365-Course/Setting-up-Office-365.htm

2.4   SIGN IN TO OFFICE 365

When you have created an account, you need to sign in to Office 365. These are the steps.

1. Open a web browser.

2. Type the web address office.com in the address field.

3. In the top right corner of the page, click on the 'Sign in' button. A Sign in wizard will open.

4. Type the e-mail address of your Office 365 account.

5. Click on 'Next'. Now your e-mail address will be analyzed. If the service can decide if it is a work or school account or a personal Microsoft account, you will be taken directly to step 7.

6. (If you are asked to select account type, select "Work or school account".)

7. Type your password.

8. Click on 'Log in'.

9. The Office 365 home page will open and you can select an app, *refer to* 2.2. above, or download desktop applications; *refer* to 4.1.

2.4.1 Stay Signed In

When you are on a secure computer, that is locked with a password or PIN, it is convenient to not have to log in each time you want to use Office 365.

The most obvious method is to let the browser save the password.

You should also answer Yes when Office 365 asks if you want to stay signed in, as this reduces the number of login occasions.

Below I describe more ways to limit the log in procedures.

2.4.1.1 Connect Windows 10 to Office 365

Each user can set Windows 10 to handle the login details to Office 365. This way the user doesn't have to log in so often, because the login details will then be used by Edge, Internet Explorer and Office.

1. In the PC, click on the Windows icon to open the start menu.

2. Click on the Settings icon and then on 'Accounts'.

3. Click on 'Connect work or school'.

4. Click on the 'Connect' button and log in to the Office 365 account.

When the connection has been established, you will see the Windows icon and the account username below the 'Connect' button, *see* the image below.

If you no longer want Windows to manage your Office 365 login, click on the account under the 'Connect' button and then on the 'Disconnect' button.

Work or school account
kate@kalmstrom.com
Manage your account

Disconnect

Demo:

https://www.kalmstrom.com/Tips/Office-365-Course/Signing-into-Office-365.htm

2.4.1.2   Single Sign-On

A very convenient way to log into Office 365 is to use the Office 365 credentials as log-in for the computer. Then the browsers Edge and Internet Explorer will pick up the log-in details, and with these browsers the user will have access to Office 365 without further log-in as soon as he/she has logged in to the computer.

2.4.1.3   Save login information

When you check the box 'Keep me signed in' at login, you must only enter the password and not the username.

If you are on a secure computer (not shared), which you lock each time you leave it, you can also make Internet Explorer save the password so that you don't have to log in at all.

It is somewhat tricky and does not work 100% of the time, but if you follow these steps, it works most of the time.

1. Go to one of your favorite Office 365 apps, such as your Mail, Calendar or SharePoint home page.

2. Set that page as your Internet Explorer home page. This is done by clicking on the Settings gear and selecting Internet Options. Under the General tab, click on the 'Use current' button at Home Page.

3. Under the Security tab, click on Local Intranet and then on the Sites button. Add the entries https://*.microsoftonline.com, https://*.outlook.com and https://*.sharepoint.com. Click Close and OK.

4. Close the browser. Then open it again and log in to Office 365, checking "Keep me signed in".

Demo:

https://www.kalmstrom.com/Tips/Office-365-Course/Save-password.htm

2.5 THE OFFICE 365 NAVIGATION BAR

In this section, we will look at how you find your way around Office 365. The navigation is managed in the navigation bar, which is present on top of the computer screen in all Office 365 apps.

2.5.1 The Left Navigation Bar

The left Office 365 navigation bar has three parts: the App Launcher or start menu, the Office 365 link, that takes you to the Office 365 start page, and the name of the current app or service.

2.5.1.1 The App Launcher

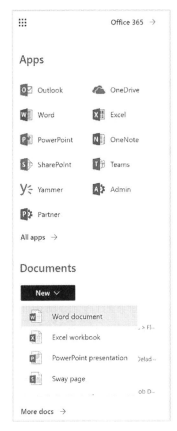

You can reach your Office 365 apps by clicking on the App Launcher in the left corner of the Office 365 navigation bar.

When you click on a tile, the corresponding app will open in the same window.

Each user will only see icons for the apps he or she has access to, but apps that are relevant to users and much used across Office 365 are emphasized.

Only administrators will see the Admin tile in the App Launcher. When you click on it, you will be directed to the Office 365 Admin Center, where you can manage the Office 365 tenant.

When you hover the mouse over an app tile, three dots will be visible. Click on them if you want to open the app in a new tab or if you want to learn more about it.

Below the app tiles, there is a button for document creation, and further below there are links to the current user's recent documents.

2.5.2 The Right Navigation Bar

The Office 365 start page has other icons on the right side of the navigation bar.

The alert icon gives alerts for reminders and new e-mails. In the settings, you can define what you want to have alerts for.

The gear icon has different content in different apps, but if you click on it in the Office 365 home page you will find your personal Office 365 settings. Here you can:

a. Change your Office 365 theme. This theme will only be shown to you, even if you are the admin of the Office 365 tenant. (A theme for the whole organization can be set in the Office 365 Admin settings.)

b. Set another start page than the default Office 365 home page. You may for example choose to show your mailbox.

c. Select which notifications you want to see in your Office 365 navigation bar and if you want to have sounds for them.

d. Change your login password.

e. Set language and time zone. (By default Office 365 will have the same regional settings as your computer)

f. Change the settings for some of your apps.

Under the question mark icon, you can find Help, Community, Legal and Privacy links.

The icon far to the right is meant to be replaced with your photo. *Refer* to 7.4.1.

Click on the image or on your name to have more options.

Peter Kalmström

Settings ✕

Search all settings 🔎

Theme

■ Default theme ⌄

Start page
Office 365 home page ⌄

Notifications
On ⌄

Password
Change your password.

Language and time zone
English (United States) ⌄

Your app settings
Office 365
Mail
Calendar
People
Yammer

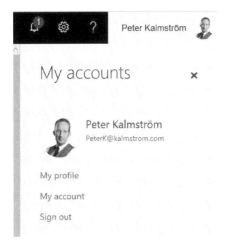

- Click on the image above 'My profile' to add your photo, or to change it.

- 'My profile', opens the Delve site, where you should add and edit information about yourself that can be seen by your colleagues; *refer to* chapter 7.

- If you click on 'My account', you can find details about your Office 365 account.

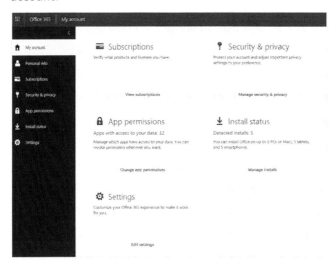

Finally, it is under your photo that you should sign out when you want to leave Office 365.

Demo:

https://www.kalmstrom.com/Tips/Office-365-Course/Office-365-Navigation-Bar.htm

2.6 FEEDBACK

Throughout Office 365, users are asked to give feedback to Microsoft. Each page has a Feedback tab in the bottom right corner, and links for Feedback are also found in other places.

The feedback forms look different in different apps, but they usually have some kind of rating. The image below comes from the Offie 365 Admin center.

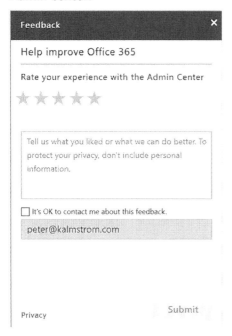

In Teams you will be directed to a forum page, and the image below comes from Stream.

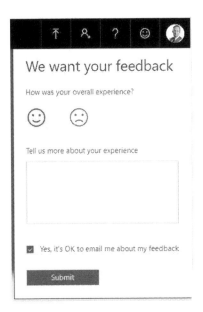

2.7 SUMMARY

After this short first chapter, you know what an Office 365 tenant and app is, how to set up your Office 365 tenant and how to navigate among the apps.

Before you can start using Office 365, you must also add more users than yourself. In next chapter we will have a look at the Office 365 Admin center, where this is done.

3 THE OFFICE 365 ADMIN CENTER

When you click on the Admin tile in the App Launcher or on office.com, you will be directed to the Office 365 Admin Center. Here administrators can manage the organization's Office 365 tenant. (Of course, only users with administrator permissions over the tenant will see the Admin tile.)

The Admin center has a left pane with various entries. It is collapsed by default, so that only the icons are visible, but here I have chosen to show the pane in expanded mode.

To go through everything in the Office 365 Admin Center would require its own book, so I will not do that here. However, I strongly recommend you to explore the Admin Center if you have permission to use it, because it is here you find almost everything needed for the management of your organization's Office 365 tenant.

You will most likely find a lot that you do not need yet, but are glad to know that it exists. One such feature is the additional security of multi-factor authentication, which is very easy to enable in Office 365; *refer to* 3.1.2.2.

3.1   USER MANAGEMENT

Each user of Office 365 has his/her own account in the organization's tenant, and to create and manage such accounts you need to be an Office 365 administrator.

Most user management is handled from the Office 365 Admin center, Users >Active Users.

3.1.1   Add Users

Office 365 user accounts can be added one by one or in a bulk. The list of all users who have been added to the tenant is sometimes referred to as "the global address book".

3.1.1.1   Create a Single User Account

These are the steps to add a single user to Office 365.

1. Click on the Admin tile on office.com or in the Office 365 App Launcher to open the Office 365 Admin center.

2. On the Admin center home page, click on 'Add a user' under the Users heading.

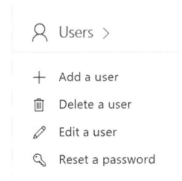

3. You can also click on the Users icon in the left pane and select 'Active users'.

4. Then click on the 'Add a user' button.

5. In the dialog that opens, enter a name, display name and user name and select country for the new user. Contact details can also be added here.

6. Select password creation method, role and licenses.

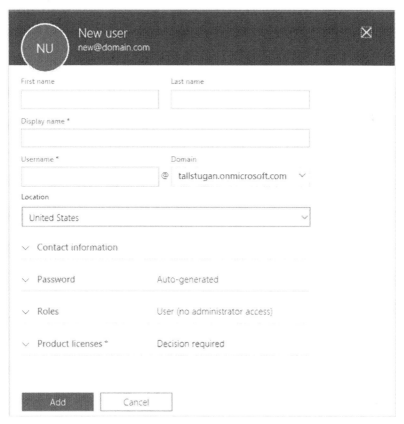

7. Click on the 'Add' button, and the user account will be created. When this is done, details for the user will be shown on the screen, and you can decide if you want to have the password sent by e-mail.

Now you can directly perform other steps, like adding the user to an Office 365 Group, *refer to* chapter 9, or adding another user. You can also do this later via the Admin center.

Demo:

https://www.kalmstrom.com/Tips/Office-365-Course/Create-Users.htm

3.1.1.2   Import Multiple Users

Instead of adding the users one by one, you can add a group of users or all users at the same time with a CSV file.

1. Open the Office 365 Admin Center.

2. Click on 'Users' and select 'Active users'.

3. Click on 'More' and select 'Import multiple users'.

4. The window that opens has two download choices:

    a. Download a CSV file with headings.

    b. Download a CSV file with headings and sample data.

5. Download one of the CSV files, open it and enter your user information, *see* below. You may of course also use another CSV file that has the correct data.

6. Upload the CSV file to Office 365.

7. Set log-in status and assign products. As this is a bulk creation, all users must be given the same status and licenses.

8. Click on Next to create the user accounts.

9. Now you can download a CSV file with all the usernames, names and temporary passwords. By default, e-mails with login details are sent out to the users, but you can uncheck that option.

Instructions for the CSV file:
If you have the user details in an Excel file or another file with a grid, put it side by side with the CSV file by using the Windows key + the right/left arrow key. Then you can copy the information in the Excel file column by column and paste it into the CSV file under suitable headings.

Each user also needs a user name. In Excel you can create all of them with a formula: =lower(B2)&"@DOMAIN", where B2 is the first name of the user and DOMAIN is the domain of your Office365 tenant.

Make sure that the CSV file deliminator is a comma by opening it in Notepad. (Replace any other deliminator with a comma and save the file again.)

Demo:

https://www.kalmstrom.com/Tips/Office-365-Course/Import-Users-CSV.htm

3.1.1.3   Add Users with a PowerShell Script

It is possible to add users to Office 365 with a PowerShell script. Scripts are re-usable and give consistency, but to fully describe the user import PowerShell script is out of scope for this book. Therefore I will just give a few hints to readers who already know PowerShell and want to try this method.

1. Download and install the Azure AD Module, if you don't already have it on your PC.

2. Run PowerShell ISE as an administrator.

3. Connect to the Azure AD which has the Office 365 user accounts.

4. Create a new user, assign license and add location and user properties.

5. Press F5 to run the script and add the user. The temporary password will be shown.

Demo:

https://www.kalmstrom.com/Tips/Office-365-Course/Add-Users-PowerShell-Azure-Ad.htm

3.1.2   Edit Users

When you need to make changes to a user account, delete or block a user or reset a password, select the user under 'Active Users' in the Office 365 Admin center and make the necessary changes in the right pane that opens.

In this pane you can also change the permission role of the user, add or remove licenses, edit e-mail and OneDrive settings and more.

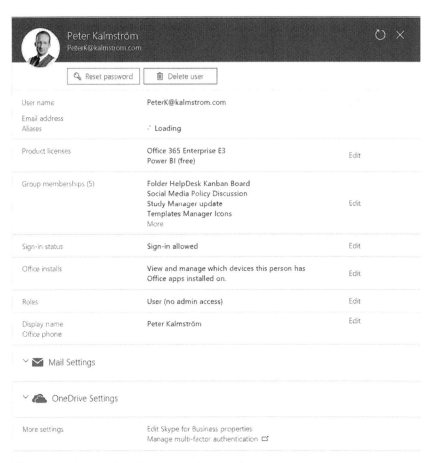

Peter Kalmström		⟳ ✕
PeterK@kalmstrom.com		

🔑 Reset password   🗑 Delete user

User name	PeterK@kalmstrom.com	
Email address		
Aliases	⋰ Loading	
Product licenses	Office 365 Enterprise E3 Power BI (free)	Edit
Group memberships (5)	Folder HelpDesk Kanban Board Social Media Policy Discussion Study Manager update Templates Manager Icons More	Edit
Sign-in status	Sign-in allowed	Edit
Office installs	View and manage which devices this person has Office apps installed on.	Edit
Roles	User (no admin access)	Edit
Display name Office phone	Peter Kalmström	Edit

∨ ✉ Mail Settings

∨ ☁ OneDrive Settings

More settings	Edit Skype for Business properties Manage multi-factor authentication ⌗

If you need to make the same change for more than one user, you can select all of them. In that case a bulk actions pane will open to the right.

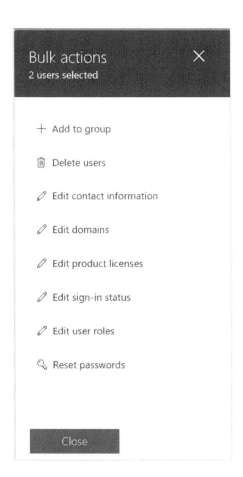

3.1.2.1   Restrict Licenses

In some cases you don't want some or all users to have access to certain apps that are included in the Office 365 subscription. When you have disabled an app, it will no longer be displayed among the tiles in the App Launcher.

3.1.2.1.1   *Restrict for All*

Some apps can be disabled for all users via Settings >Apps. Select the app you want to disable and turn it off.

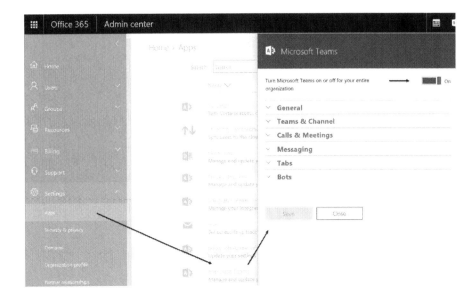

3.1.2.1.2 *Restrict for Specific Users*

To restrict the use of one or more apps for a specific user, select that user among the active users in the Office 365 Admin settings. In the right pane that opens, click on 'Edit' at 'Product licenses'.

Click on the expand icon to the left of the license name.

Now you can see all included apps and disable the ones that should not be available to this user.

∧   Office 365 Enterprise E3   ▮▮▮▮▯ On

6 of 25 licenses available

Flow for Office 365   ▮▮▮▮▯ On

PowerApps for Office 365   ▮▮▮▮▯ On

Microsoft Teams   ▮▮▮▮▯ On

Microsoft Planner   ▮▮▮▮▯ On

Sway   ▮▮▮▮▯ On

Mobile Device Management for Office 365 (These   ▮▯▯▯▯ Off
licenses do not need to be individually assigned)

Yammer Enterprise   ▮▮▮▮▯ On

Azure Rights Management   ▮▮▮▮▯ On

Office 365 ProPlus   ▮▮▮▮▯ On

Skype for Business Online (Plan 2)   ▮▮▮▮▯ On

Office Online   ▮▮▮▮▯ On

SharePoint Online (Plan 2)   ▮▮▮▮▯ On

Exchange Online (Plan 2)   ▮▮▮▮▯ On

∧   Power BI (free)   ▮▮▮▮▯ On

Unlimited licenses available

Power BI (free)   ▮▮▮▮▯ On

3.1.2.2   Multi-factor Authentication

It is easy to add multi-factor authentication to Office 365-accounts if you want more security than just a username and a password. If you enable multi-factor authentication, users can, for example, get an SMS message with a code to verify their identity, in addition to the username and password.

1. Open the Office 365 Admin Center and select Users >Active Users >More and 'Setup Azure multi-factor auth'.

2. A page will open, with a list of all users. This page also has a link to the multi-factor authentication guide, which I recommend you to study.

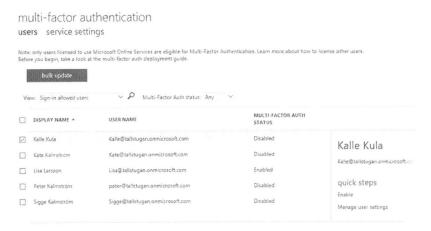

3. Select specific users that should be required multi-factor authentication or select all users. You can also bulk update the authentication settings with a CSV file, in a similar way as when you added the users, *refer to* 3.1.1.2.

4. Under 'quick steps' click on 'Enable'.

5. In the dialog box that opens, click on 'enable multi-factor auth'.

6. You will now get a confirmation that the multi-factor authentication has been enabled for the selected user(s).

7. Next time a selected user logs into Office 365, he/she needs to complete the multi-factor authentication and select which option for the extra authentication should be used.

For added security, we need to further verify your account

Your admin has required that you set up this account for additional security verification.

Set it up now

Sign out and sign in with a different account

More information

3.1.3   Office 365 Permissions

Office 365 comes with a set of administrator roles that can be assigned to users. Each admin role gives permission to perform specific tasks in the Office 365 Admin center.

3.1.3.1   Global Administrator

The person who signs up for an Office 365 subscription by default becomes the Global administrator, and he or she is the only person who can assign other admin roles. But one of the roles that can be assigned is Global admin, so there can still be more than one global administrator for a tenant.

I recommend that you have more than one Global administrator but not too many, to minimize security risks. Make sure that all global administrators give a mobile number and an alternate e-mail address in their contact information.

3.1.3.2   Assign Admin Role

Global administrators can assign admin roles to any of the tenant's users in the Office 365 Admin center >Users >Active users.

1. Select the user you want to give an admin role.

2. In the right pane that opens, click on the Edit button at 'Roles'.

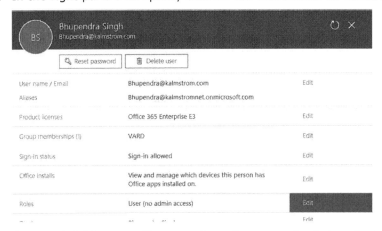

3. A second right pane will open, where the current role is selected.

4. Select another radio button, either 'Global administrator' or 'Customized administrator'. For both the 'Global administrator' and the 'Customized administrator' options you are asked to give an alternate e-mail address. It should be a domain outside your company, for example 'outlook.com', so that the user can be reached if the company domain should fail.

When you select 'Customized administrator' you will have various choices. Check the box for one or several of them.

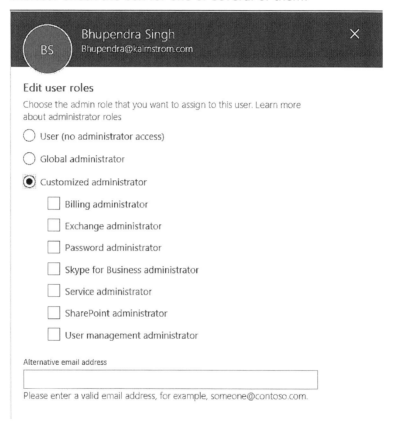

5. Save the change when you are finished.

3.2 UPDATES

Microsoft uses a rolling release model for the Office 365 platform, and the service components are updated often. This means that subscribers receive new product updates and features as they become available and without paying anything extra.

You can manage how your organization receives these updates:

- Sign up for Targeted Release, earlier called First Release, so that your organization receives updates first.

- Designate that only certain individuals receive the early updates.

- Use the default Standard release schedule and receive the updates when they are released broadly to all Office 365 subscribers.

The Targeted Release options give a possibility to help shape the product by providing early feedback. The default option, on the other hand, gives administrators extra time to prepare support staff and users for upcoming changes.

I recommend that you let some users have the Targeted Releases, to see what they are about, how they will affect the organization and if there are bugs. The majority of users can wait until the new feature is released to all.

There are good possibilities to know beforehand what updates are in line:

1. For significant updates, subscribers are first notified by the Office 365 public roadmap at http://fasttrack.microsoft.com/roadmap.

2. As an update gets closer to rolling out, it is communicated through each organization's Office 365 >Admin center >Health >Message Center.

3.2.1 Set up Targeted Release

The Targeted Release option is set in the Office 365 Admin center >Settings >Organization profile. Click on 'Actions' and select 'Edit' at 'Release preferences'.

A right pane will open. Select the radio button for Targeted Release for everyone or for selected users. Click Next.

Release preferences

Release track

○ Standard release
   Get updates when we release them broadly.

○ Targeted release for everyone
   Get updates early for your entire organization

● Targeted release for selected users
   Pick people to preview updates so that you can prepare your organization

[Next]   [Cancel]

You are first asked to confirm your choice, and then you can add the selected users who should have the Targeted Release – if you have selected that option. Check the box for the selected users, or start writing in the search field to have suggestions. Click on Save to finalize.

3.3   SPECIFIC ADMIN CENTERS

When you expand the 'Admin centers' entry in the left pane, you will find entries to some specific admin centers and to the Azure portal. Security and Compliance information and settings are also found here.

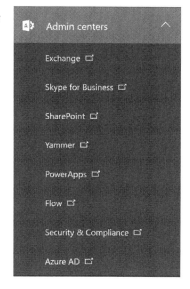

I will describe two of the specific Admin centers below, but the rest of them will be described in connection with the app or service they belong to.

Apps and services that don't have a dedicated Admin center can often be managed via >Settings >Services & add-ins.

3.3.1 The Security & Compliance Center

The Security & Compliance center is the Office 365 portal for data protection. It has its own tile in the App Launcher, and the Security & Compliance Center is also one of the Specific Admin Centers you can reach from the Office 365 Admin center.

In the Security & Compliance center, global administrators or administrators appointed by a global administrator can manage data protection and compliance issues and audit user activity.

In the center of the home page you can find a description of some of the headings in the left pane. The right pane has recommendations based on the tenant's data and settings.

This is what you can view and manage in the Security & Compliance center:

- Alerts.

- Permissions for the Security & Compliance center.

- Threat management. Here you can set up rules for the users' mobile devices, set up data loss prevention and configure spam filters.

- Data governance. Here you can import e-mail from other systems, enable archive mailboxes and set policies for content retention.

- Search & investigation of user activity.

- Reports on data and activity.

- Service assurance details from Microsoft.

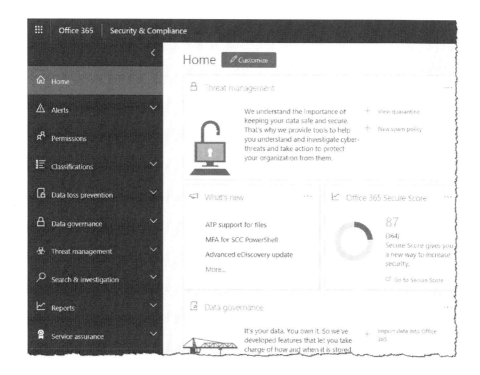

3.3.2 Azure Active Directory

Office 365 uses the cloud-based user authentication service
Azure Active Directory, or Azure AD. It does not have its
own tile in the App Launcher, but Azure AD is another one
of the Specific Admin Centers you can reach from the Office
365 Admin center.

The Office 365 user accounts are stored in the Azure AD, but normally
administrators create and manage users in the Office 365 Admin center.
However, users can be managed in Azure Active Directory too, and
Azure AD also gives other possibilities that are out of scope for this
book.

If you want to explore Azure Active Directory, I recommend you to use
the 'Quick start' option and study the information there.

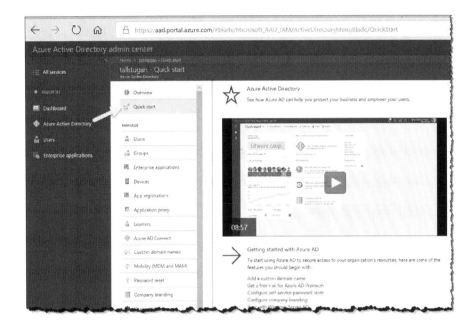

3.4 SUMMARY

Now you have had an introduction to the Office 365 Admin center, and you know how to add and manage users and how to give special permissions. I have also given a few examples on what you can do in the Admin center, but will come back to the Office 365 Admin center later in this book. Now it is time to start using your organization's new tenant!

4 OFFICE 365 USERS

This chapter has information about what ordinary users can do to personalize their Office 365 accounts. I describe how each user can download and install additional apps that do not run in the cloud but on PCs or mobile devices.

I also explain how users can select Office edition to work with and some advantages with the online editions, and you will learn how to share an Office 365 mailbox and add it to a desktop Outlook.

4.1 DOWNLOADS

Desktop and mobile apps for each user are included in most Office 365 Business and Enterprise plans.

4.1.1 Office ProPlus

The Microsoft Office suite has been on the market for many years and includes the most common applications for word processing, calculation, presentations and notes. The Office 365 Enterprise subscriptions include the Office 365 ProPlus, which is the Office desktop suit, and also online editions of Word, Excel, PowerPoint and OneNote.

Office 365 ProPlus includes Word, Excel, PowerPoint, OneNote, Access, Publisher, Outlook, Skype for Business and OneDrive for Business.

The Office suite is well known, and I will not go into a description of the included apps here. Each of them have a lot of features and deserves their own book. For Excel, please refer to my *Excel 2016 from Scratch*.

Below I will only give a short presentation of OneNote, which might be a bit less known, and explain how to add Visio to an Office 365 license.

4.1.1.1 Installation

There are three ways to download and install the Office desktop editions. The first option starts the download, while the other two takes you to a Software page where you can make choices and also download other software.

- On the Office 365 Home page, click on the 'Install Office 2016' button in the top right corner. The installation file starts downloading at once,

45

and there are no choices to make. You will have the language of your Office 365 account.

- Click on the 'Other installs' link and then select to install the Office suite.

- Click on the Settings gear on any page in Office 365 and open the Office 365 settings. Then open the Software section.

When you select an option that takes you to the Software page, *see* the image below, you may select language, and you can repeat the process and install more than one language, if you for example need spell checking in multiple languages. It will still count as one installation. The Software page also gives other download options.

Click on 'Install' when you have made your choice.

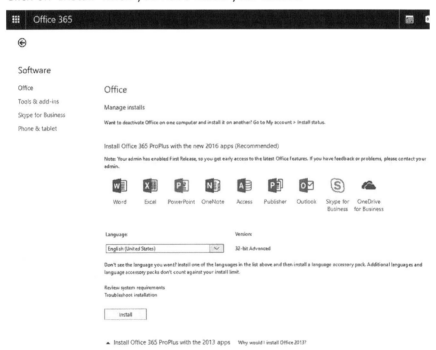

The rest of the process is the same for all three methods.

1. Click on 'Run' in the download message at the bottom of the screen.

2. A dialog will open. Click on 'Yes' to allow the changes, and the installation will start.

4.1.1.2   Activation

When the installation is finished, open one of the Office desktop applications and sign in to activate your desktop Office.

The activation gives you upgrades and a possibility to save files to OneDrive and SharePoint. Links to your default SharePoint site will be added to the 'Save As' pane in the applications.

You have to be connected to the internet for Microsoft's monthly license check. If no license can be found, you will still be able to read existing files, but you cannot edit them or create new files. This mode is called "limited functionality mode".

Demo:

https://www.kalmstrom.com/Tips/Office-365-Course/Installing-Office-365-Pro-Plus.htm

4.1.1.3   Select Edition

The Online editions of the Office apps do not have as many features as the desktop editions, but sometimes they are more convenient to use. Here we will have a look at how users can select which Office edition to use.

When you open a file from anywhere in Office 365, it opens in the Online edition by default. For example, if you click on an attached Word document in an e-mail in the Outlook Web App (OWA), the file will be opened in Word Online.

You can, however, always select to open the document in the client version of Word instead. The image below shows some important controls in Word Online, and the other online editions have similar features.

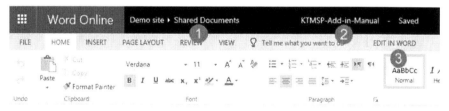

1. To save and return to the library, click on 'Shared Documents'.

2. To change the file name, from the default 'Document' into something that better describes the file content, click on the default name and write the new name.

3. To work in the desktop version instead, click on 'EDIT IN WORD'.

4.1.1.4   Editing by Multiple Users

Several people can work on the same Word Online, Excel Online or PowerPoint Online file at the same time. This can be done if the file is stored in a shared library or folder:

- A SharePoint library, where all files are shared between everyone who has access to the library. This SharePoint library may of course be a library used by an Office 365 group, *refer to* chapter 9.

- A shared OneDrive folder, *refer to* 8.2.

When you open a document and another person is editing the same document, you will have a message about it:

You can also see where in the document the other user is working.

You can continue your editing, because all changes, no matter which one of the users who made them, will be visible in the document.

You can be more than two users on the same document. I have seen examples on around 15 people collaborating on a document in Word Online!

If you want to send a link to the file you want to cooperate on, click on the Share button in the navigation bar of the Office Online file.

Demo:

https://www.kalmstrom.com/Tips/SharePoint-Online-Course/Word-Offline-Overview.htm

4.1.1.5   OneNote

The OneNote tile in the Office 365 App Launcher or on the office.com start page opens the Online version of OneNote, Microsoft's note-taking tool that is part of the Office package. (OneNote can also be opened from SharePoint.)

In OneNote you take the notes on pages. Each page has a heading, and they are grouped in sections. Create new page or section by right clicking on a section.

When you open OneNote Online via the Notebook link in the Quick Launch, you will have various options to insert text, images and links.

Under the tabs you can find controls similar to the Word controls but also special OneNote controls, like 'Tag' and 'Meeting Details'.

Office 365 Groups come with links to a shared OneNote site, and SharePoint team sites have a 'Notebook' link in the left side navigation (the Quick Launch) that opens OneNote Online.

OneNote works well in the browser, and with OneNote in SharePoint and Groups, users can share notes easily.

The default OneNote notebook and all other notebooks you create, are stored in each SharePoint team site's Site Assets library. You can reach all the team site's notebooks by clicking on 'Notebook's at the top left in OneNote Online.

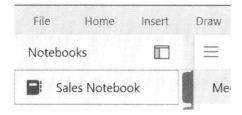

Demo:

https://www.kalmstrom.com/Tips/SharePoint-Online-Course/OneNote.htm

4.1.2   Other Installs

Via the 'Other installs' link on office.com you can install more apps. The options are displayed in the left pane of the page that opens.

- Under 'Tools & add-ins', you can find Microsoft's Support and Recovery Assistant and the 2013 (and last) version of InfoPath and SharePoint Designer.

Tools & add-ins

Microsoft Support and Recovery Assistant for Office 365

Get help troubleshooting and fixing problems you might run into using Outlook or Office 36!

Install

InfoPath 2013

Use InfoPath 2013 to design sophisticated electronic forms that help you quickly and cost-effectively gather information.

Download and install

SharePoint Designer 2013

Use SharePoint Designer 2013 to create workflows and modify the look and feel of your SharePoint sites.

SharePoint Designer 2013 Download and install

Install SharePoint Designer 2013 SP1.

- Skype for Business is included in the desktop Office suite, but under 'Skype for Business' you may also download Skype for Business 2015 and the Skype for Business Web Scheduler (to be used for Skype for Business meetings when you don't have Outlook or Windows).

- To see and download phone and tablet editions of Office 365 apps, click on 'Phone & tablet' and select the smart device you want to use.

Software

Office

Tools & add-ins

Skype for Business

Phone & tablet

Choose your phone or tablet

Phone	Tablet
Windows Phone	Windows tablet
Windows 10 Mobile	iPad
iPhone	Android tablet
Android phone	
BlackBerry®	
Nokia (Symbian OS)	
Other	

When you have clicked on a link to choose a smart device, you can get the available apps for that device.

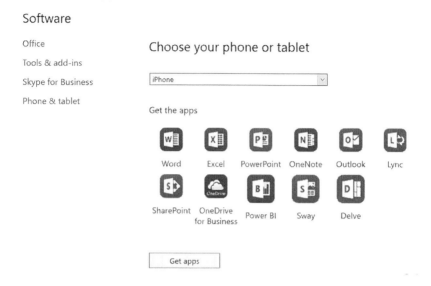

4.1.3 Add Visio to Office 365

Microsoft Visio is a diagramming and vector graphics application that helps you create professional diagrams that are linked to data and updated when data changes.

Visio is part of the Microsoft Office family, but it is not included in the basic Office 365 packages. Organizations have to pay an extra fee to use Visio regularly, but you can try Visio without cost and see if it is useful to you.

Visio has two subscription levels, Plan 1 and Plan 2. Plan 2 includes the Visio desktop app.

Below are the steps for a Plan 2 trial, but if you want to buy directly step 1-3 are the same. The steps for Plan 1 are similar, but there is of course no application installation.

1. Open the Office 365 Admin center >Billing >Purchase services.

2. Use Ctrl + F to search for Visio.

3. Find the 'Visio Online Plan 2' which has a free trial.

4. Click on 'Start free trial'.

5. Click on 'Continue' when the trial is set up.

order receipt

Your confirmation number is: 312a1775-a31f-469a-8325-bbf5f0eb3468
Important: To use your new licenses, make sure to assign them by editing
users on the Users page.

Continue

Once the trial set up, you must assign the subscription to users. This can be done in two ways:

- Wizard:

1. When you click on 'Continue' in the order receipt, *see* the image above, you will be directed to the Office 365 home page. Click on the new 'Go to setup' button.

2. Now you will be asked to add users who should have access to Visio.

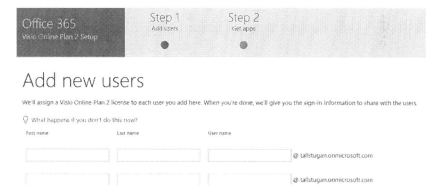

3. Click on Next.

4. Now you will be asked to install the Visio application for yourself. When you click on 'Install now', you will be directed to your Software page, see below.

- Quick:

1. Go to 'Active users', check the boxes for the users you want to assign Visio to and bulk add the new license to them.

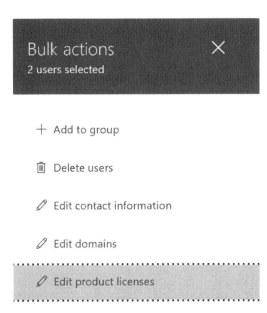

2. Add to the existing licenses.

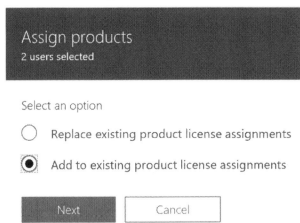

3. Turn on the Visio licenses for the selected users.

Users who have been assigned Visio can now download and install the desktop application by clicking on 'View account' under his/her Office 365 profile picture. This will take them to the Software page, which now has a new Visio entry.

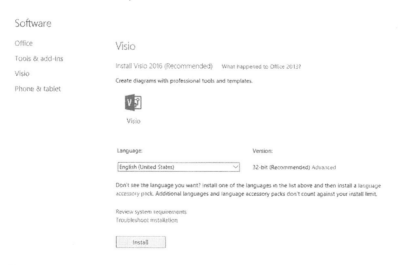

Demo:

https://www.kalmstrom.com/Tips/Office-365-Course/Add-Visio.htm

4.2 PERSONAL MAILBOX

Included in each Office 365 account is a personal mailbox with apps for e-mail, calendar, contacts (also called People) and tasks.

Each user can reach his or her four mailbox apps via office.com or the App Launcher. The apps can also be reached from within one of the apps, via the icons at the bottom left corner of the page.

4.2.1 Share the Mailbox

Each mailbox owner can give permission to other people to use the mailbox.

1. Right click on the mailbox in Outlook Web Access and select 'Permissions…'.

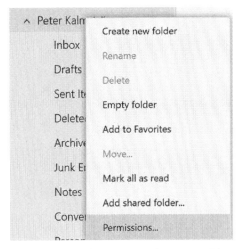

2. Click on the plus sign and start writing a name. Select the correct name among the suggestions.

3. Set the permissions you wish to grant the new user on the mailbox by selecting a level in the dropdown or by checking the boxes for a custom level.

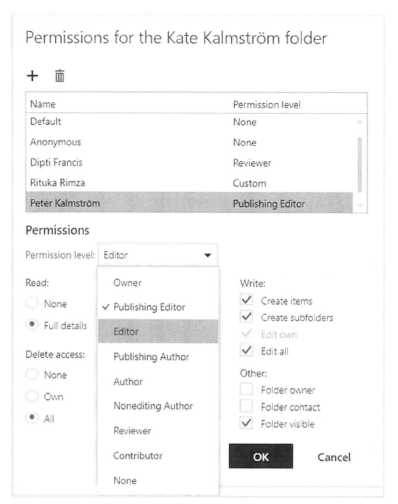

Permissions for the Kate Kalmström folder

Remove additional users by selecting the name and clicking on the waste basket above the names.

4.2.2 Use OWA in Local Outlook

By default, you can only use your personal Office 365 mailbox in the browser edition of Outlook. It is called Outlook Web App, or OWA. However, when you have downloaded the Office desktop editions to your PC, it is a good idea to add the Office 365 mailbox to your desktop Outlook also.

When you add your personal Office 365 mailbox to your local Outlook, you can work with your Office 365 mail in your PC too, even if you are not connected to the internet. Your local PC will synchronize with OWA once you are online again.

The steps below is for a PC with Windows 10, where Windows has been set to manage the Office 365 login details; *refer to* 2.4.1.1.

If you have a lower Windows version, or if you have not connected your Windows 10 to Office 365, you can still use the instruction below. You must then enter your Office 365 e-mail address and login details.

1. Open Outlook on your PC.

2. If it is the first time you use Outlook, answer Yes to connect to an e-mail account.

   If you are already using Outlook with another account, click on 'Add account, under the File tab, and enter the e-mail address of your Office 365 account.

3. Enter your password to have the connection established. Outlook will now start searching for the Office 365 account.

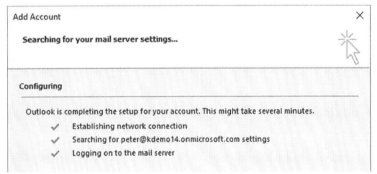

4. Click on 'Finish' when the setup is completed and you see three green check marks like in the image above.

4.2.2.1   Settings

By default, Office 2013 and 2016 saves e-mails from the last 12 months on the computer, to make it fast.

To change this setting, open the Account Settings under the 'File' tab in your local Outlook and select the account that you want to change. Click on 'Change'.

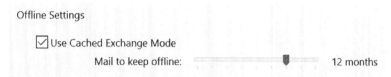

Make sure that the box for 'Use Cached Exchange Mode' is checked. Drag the bar to the desired value. Click on 'Next' and 'Finish'. The change will take effect when you have restarted Outlook.

Demo:

https://www.kalmstrom.com/Tips/Office-365-Course/Set-Up-Outlook-With-Office-365.htm

4.3   SUMMARY

Office 365 subscriptions include client apps that users can download. In this chapter I have explained how everyone can take advantage of the desktop editions of the Office suite and of mobile apps for various products.

We have looked at how you can switch between the online and the desktop edition of the Office apps, and you have learned how multiple users can work on the same document at the same time.

I have also described how users can share their personal Office 365 mailboxes and how such a mailbox can be added to a local Outlook.

Finally I gave a presentation of OneNote and explained how it is connected to SharePoint and Office 365 Groups, and described how to add Visio to the Office 365 subscription or trial.

These were some of the apps that each Office 365 user can manage him/herself. In the chapters about Delve and OneDrive, you can learn more about personal usage of Office 365.

Each user also has a personal SharePoint site collection, which we will look at in chapter 8, OneDrive for Business.

5 EXCHANGE

Microsoft Exchange is a Windows server for e-mail, calendars and contacts lists. E-mailing is mission critical for most organizations, but managing growing mailbox sizes has always been a bit of a nightmare for IT-departments. Therefore, the stability and security of Office 365 is appreciated, and a wish to use Exchange Online for e-mail management is often one of the driving reasons when an organization decides on an Office 365 subscription.

The 50 GB default mailbox size is popular, as well as the unlimited archival options. Still, the online Exchange edition that is included in Office 365 has some limitations compared to the server edition. I will not go into them here, but you can study them at https://technet.microsoft.com/en-us/library/exchange-online-limits.aspx.

Many organizations prefer to combine the Exchange on-premises and online options in a hybrid deployment, to overcome limitations or for a smooth transfer to Exchange Online.

5.1 THE EXCHANGE ADMIN CENTER

Global and Exchange administrators can reach the Exchange Admin center from the left panel in the Office 365 Admin center.

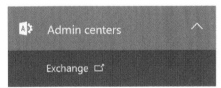

In the Exchange Admin center you can manage the tenant's mailboxes. Here I will just give a few examples on the possibilities. (For even more options, use the Azure Active Directory; *refer to* 3.3.2.)

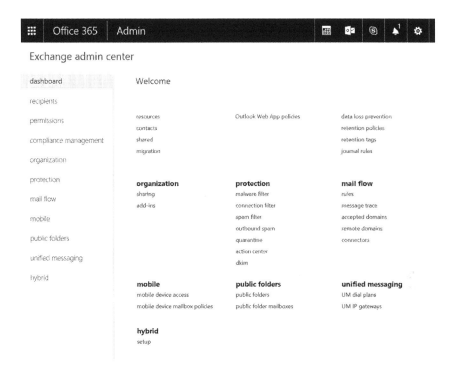

5.2   PERSONAL MAILBOXES

When you create a new Office 365 user, *refer to* 3.1.1, and assign an Exchange Online licence to that user, a mailbox is automatically created for the user.

These mailboxes can be centrally managed in the Exchange Admin center, just like all the other mailboxes within the tenant.

Select the user/mailbox and make necessary changes in the right pane.

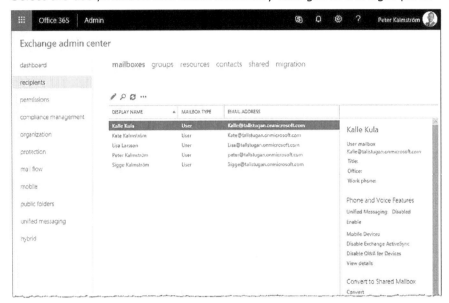

For more edit possibilities, click on the edit icon above the list of display names, or double click on the selected mailbox, and make changes in the dialog that opens.

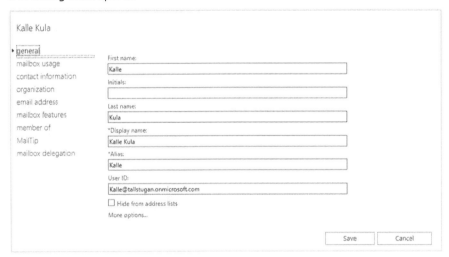

5.2.1   Share a Personal Mailbox

By default only the user for whom the mailbox was created has access to it, but the Exchange admin can give more people access to the mailbox and let them send e-mails from it. An assistant can for example be allowed to handle a manager's calendar or send e-mails in the name of a manager. (The mailbox owner can also share his/her mailbox from OWA; *refer to* 4.2.1.)

This is how an Exchange administrator can add more users to a mailbox from within the Exchange Admin center:

1. Select a mailbox and doubleclick on it, or click on the edit icon above the list of mailboxes.

2. Select 'mailbox delegation' in the left hand panel.

3. Click on the plus sign above one of the boxes to add more users.

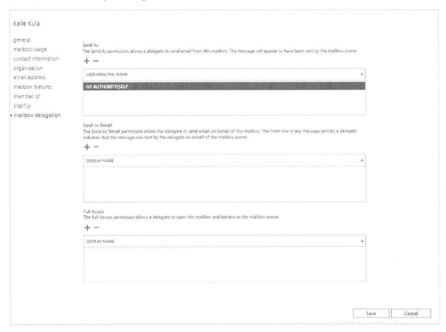

The additional users can be removed again, by using the minus sign, but the original user cannot be removed from the mailbox. The only way to remove the original user from the mailbox is to delete the account.

5.3   SHARED MAILBOXES AND PUBLIC FOLDERS

A shared mailbox and a public Outlook folder in a public folder mailbox, can be used by several people. It allows a group of users to view and send e-mails from a common mailbox.

The shared mailbox/public folder can provide a generic e-mail address for contacts with your company or organization, for example support@company.com. With a common e-mail address for all e-mails of the same kind, the e-mail management will become easier and more efficient.

A public folder is just a mail enabled folder. There is no calendar, contacts or tasks. When you create a shared mailbox, on the other hand, all the "extras" will be created automatically and shared among the users who have access to the mailbox.

There is one more possibility to share a mailbox: create a user account for a non existing user, for example Support + the company name. Then add users to the auto-created mailbox, *see* above.

However, when you use this method and create a user account, that "user" requires an Exchange Online license, which incurs a cost. A shared mailbox/public folder does not require an additional license and is therefore essentially free of charge.

5.3.1   Create a Public Folder

A public folder must be contained in a public folder mailbox, so if you don't already have a public folder mailbox you must create one. The first public folder mailbox you create is known as the primary public folder mailbox, and it contains the only writable copy of the public folder hierarchy. After the primary public folder mailbox has been created, you can create public folders.

When the public folder has been created and mailbox enabled, and users have been added, the people who have access to the folder can add it to any Outlook Web App or desktop Outlook within the organization.

5.3.1.1 Create a Public Folder Mailbox

The public folder mailbox is created from the Exchange Admin center dashboard.

1. Click on 'public folder mailboxes'.

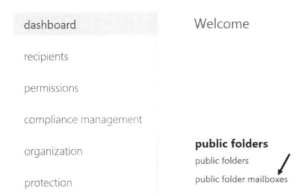

2. Click on the plus sign to create a new public folder mailbox.

3. Give the new mailbox a name.

4. Click on Save.

5. You will now see the newly created mailbox in the list of public folder mailboxes.

5.3.1.2 Create a public folder

You can continue with the public folder creation right after the creation of a public folder mailbox, on the same page.

1. Select 'public folders' in the top navigation.

public folders   public folder mailboxes

2. Click on the plus sign to create a new public folder.

3. Enter a name for the public folder. This is the name that will be visible in Outlook. You don't have to enter anything in the Path field.

new public folder

*Name:

Path:

\

4. Click on Save.

5. Now you will see the new public folder in the folders list. In the right pane, Click on 'Enable' to enable the Mail settings.

In-house Support

Path: \In-house Support
Total items: 0
Modified: 2016-12-18 08:08
Size (MB): 0

Mail settings - Disabled

Enable

Folder permissions

Manage

6. The e-mail address is auto-generated from the mailbox name, but you can edit the address in the public folder settings, 'e-mail address'.

7. Click on 'Manage', *see* image at point 5 above, to open a dialog that lets you add people who should have access to the public folder.

8. Add users to whom you want to give access to the public folder. When you want to give access to many users, create a user group and select the group just as you select regular users.

   a. Click on the plus sign.

   b. Click on Browse. A dialog with the tenant's Office 365 users and groups will be displayed. Select one of them and click OK. It is not possible to select multiple users/groups at the same time.

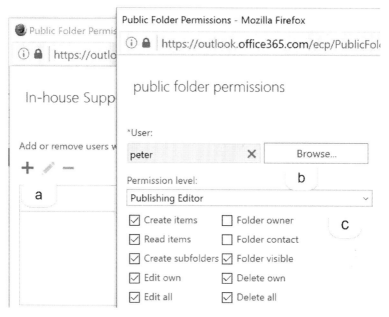

c. Give the selected user or group a suitable permission over the public folder.

d. Click Save and then Save again when you have added the users.

e. Click on Close when the operation is completed.

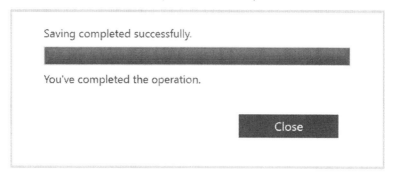

5.3.1.1 Add a public folder to OWA

When users add the public folder to Outlook Web App, they can work with the e-mails in a web browser.

1. Click on the Outlook icon in the Office 365 navigation to open Outlook.

2. In the folders list, right click on Favorites.

3. Click on 'Add public folder to Favorites'.

4. Select the public folder you want to add and click on 'Add to Favorites'.

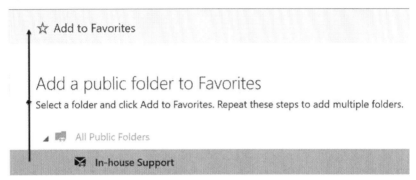

5.3.2   Create a Shared Mailbox

A shared mailbox can be created as a new mailbox, but you can also convert a regular mailbox into a shared mailbox. Select the user/mailbox and click on 'Convert' under 'Convert to Shared Mailbox' in the right panel.

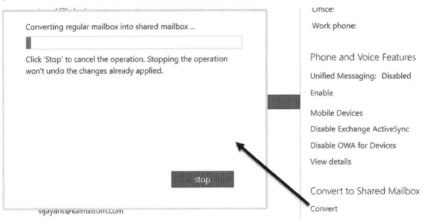

These are the steps to create a new shared mailbox:

1. Click on 'shared' under 'recipients' in the The Exchange Admin center dashboard.

Exchange admin center

dashboard	**Welcome**
recipients	
permissions	**recipients**
	mailboxes
compliance management	groups
	resources
organization	contacts
	shared

2. Click on the plus sign to create a new shared mailbox. Fill out the display name and the first part of the e-mail address.

mailboxes   groups   resources   contacts   **shared**   migration

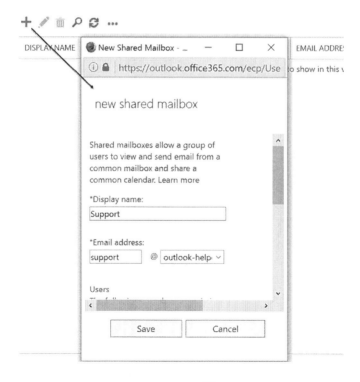

new shared mailbox

Shared mailboxes allow a group of users to view and send email from a common mailbox and share a common calendar. Learn more

*Display name:

Support

*Email address:

support   @   outlook-help ∨

Users

Save   Cancel

3. Make sure the display name is user-friendly, so that people recognize what it is. The display name will appear

   a. in the Exchange address book

   b. in the To field in e-mails sent to the address of the shared mailbox

   c. in the From field in e-mails sent from the shared mailbox

   d. in the list of mailboxes on the Shared page in the Exchange Admin center.

4. Click on the plus sign to add the people or groups who should have access to the mailbox.

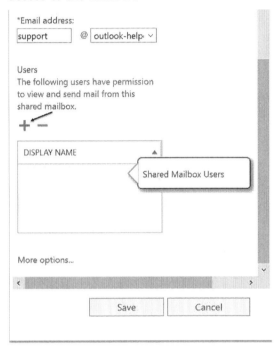

5. A new dialog with the names of all Office 365 users and groups will open.

   a. Hold down the Crtl key and click on all names that you want to include.

   b. Click on 'Add'.

   c. Click OK.

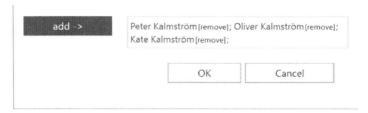

6. Click on Save.

If you want to change users or groups for the mailbox later, open the 'shared' page again and edit the mailbox. Click on 'mailbox delegation' in the left panel and then on the plus or minus signs to add or remove users.

When you want to give access to many users, create a user group. It will be visible in the list of users, and you can select the group just as you select regular users.

5.3.2.1 Add a Shared Mailbox to OWA

When users add the shared mailbox to Outlook Web App, they can work with the e-mails in a web browser.

1. Click on the Outlook icon in the Office 365 navigation to open Outlook.

2. In the folders list, right click on the mailbox name and select 'Add shared folder...'.

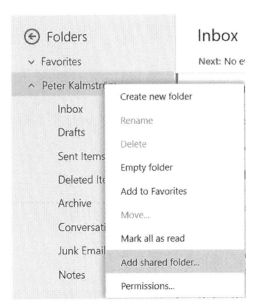

3. Start writing the name of the shared mailbox you want to add and select the correct option from the suggestions.

4. Click on 'Add'.

5. Send from Shared Mailbox/Public Folder in OWA.

When you have added a shared mailbox to your personal Outlook Web Access, you probably want to send some e-mails using the shared mailbox e-mail address as reply address instead of your personal address. OWA gives you a possibility to make a choice of reply address:

1. Reply to an e-mail, or click on '+ New' to send a new e-mail. (It does not matter which mailbox you do it from.)

2. Click on the ellipsis and select 'Show From'.

3. The first time you do this, you have to find the shared mailbox address.

   a. Right click on your personal e-mail address in the From field and select 'Remove'.

   b. Start writing the e-mail address of the shared mailbox and select the correct one among the suggestions.

The next time you can select reply address by clicking on the arrow to the right of 'From'.

5.3.2.2   Add a Shared Mailbox to Desktop Outlook

Users who have been added to a shared mailbox or public folder might prefer to use the mailbox in their local Outlook (included in Office) instead of working in the browser.

A public folder will show up in the user's local Outlook automatically, and a shared mailbox might also show up automatically. However, depending on profile and settings it is sometimes necessary to add the shared mailboxes to Outlook manually.

This can be done in different ways. The additional account and additional mailbox options give the whole shared mailbox, with calendar and contacts. The third option will only give one folder, such as the inbox, contacts or calendar.

5.3.2.2.1   *Add as Additional Account*

The easiest way to add the shared mailbox to Outlook is to add it as an additional account, in the same way as you do when you add your personal Office 365 account to your local Outlook; *refer to* 4.2.2.

1. In Outlook, open the File tab.

2. Click on Add Account.

3. Fill out your name and Office 365 user name and type your Office 365 password twice.

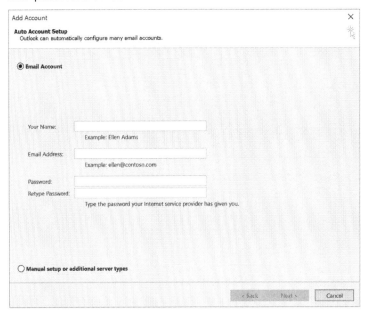

4. Click Next.

5. Now Outlook starts searching for the mailbox where you have been added.

6. Click Finish when the connection has been established.

7. Restart Outlook. Now you can see the shared mailbox or public folder among your other mailboxes and use it in the same way as you use your personal mailbox.

5.3.2.2.2   *Add as Additional Mailbox*

To add the shared mailbox as an additional mailbox, open the Outlook 'File' tab and select Info >Account Settings >Account Settings...

1. Click on 'Change'.

2. Click on 'More settings' and then select the 'Advanced' tab.

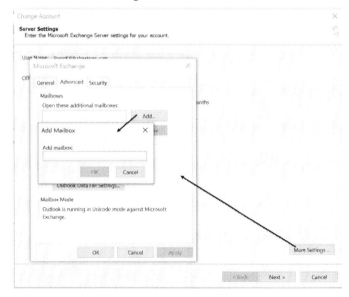

3. Click on 'Add' and type in the name of the shared mailbox.

4. Click on OK, Next and Finish.

5.3.2.2.3 *Other User's Folder*

If you only want to open a shared mailbox in Outlook temporarily, you can use the 'Other User's Folder' option.

1. Go to File >Open & Export >Other User's Folder.

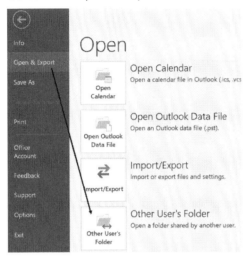

2. Click on 'Name' and select the mailbox you want to open.

3. Click OK.

4. The mailbox will open and you can send to and from it.

5.3.2.3   Send from Shared Mailbox/Public Folder in Outlook

The first time you want to send from the shared mailbox/public folder in a desktop Outlook, click on the arrow at 'From' and select 'Other E-mail Address...'

Click on 'From' and select the mailbox you want to send from.

Next time, the shared mailbox/public folder e-mail address will show up among the choices under the 'From' arrow.

If you don't see the 'From field' in your e-mail messages, Search for 'From', select 'From Field' and right click. Now you can select to add the From field to the Quick Access Toolbar.

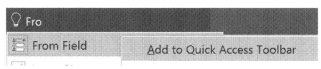

Demo:

https://www.kalmstrom.com/Tips/Office-365-Course/Shared-Mailbox.htm

5.4   SUMMARY

Exchange and its mailboxes is one of the most important parts of Office 365. As Office 365 is a sharing platform, this chapter has mostly dealt with the creation and sharing of personal and shared mailboxes and public folders. Most of this is done in the Exchange Admin center, so I hope the introduction given in this chapter has made it feel familiar, so that you can continue exploring it on your own.

Next chapter is also about a heavy Office 365 component: SharePoint Online.

6 SHAREPOINT

SharePoint is Microsoft's platform for enterprise content management and sharing. The cloud edition of SharePoint is called SharePoint Online. It is included in most Office 365 subscriptions, and you need to subscribe to Office 365 to use SharePoint Online.

Office 365 Groups and several apps use SharePoint in the background, so you can reach SharePoint content from these apps and not only from the App Launcher and from office.com.

In this chapter, we will look at how SharePoint is built and how you can move around among sites and apps. I will describe:

- How information can be shared in SharePoint

- The outline of the SharePoint architecture

- How to reach the SharePoint admin center

- How to create site collections, sites, pages and apps

- How to find the contents of a site

- The default content of a team site

- The modern and classic experience in sites, pages and apps

- What we mean by a SharePoint app

- How content can be added to a SharePoint library

Here I can only give a short overview of SharePoint, and my focus lies on what you need to know to use SharePoint with other Office 365 apps. For a detailed description of the possibilities that SharePoint Online give, refer to my book *SharePoint Online from Scratch*, which is available from Amazon.

6.1 SHARING

One of the most important reasons for using SharePoint is that you want to share information and documents within a company or an organization. These are the most common sharing methods:

- Create a new document directly in a SharePoint library, or upload an existing document.

- Add info to a SharePoint list, for example a team tasks list or a team calendar.

- Use the Newsfeed on the home page of the SharePoint team site. Create a new entry, like or reply to an existing entry or upload an image or tag someone.

- Add or edit SharePoint pages. You can fill your pages with text, images, links or videos and insert tables, app parts and web parts.

Demo:

https://kalmstrom.com/Tips/SharePoint-Online-Course/Share-Info-In-SharePoint.htm

6.2   SITES

SharePoint is built as a hierarchy, where the highest level in the Office 365 tenant consists of multiple SharePoint site collections, and where the lowest level is the list item column values.

The core of the SharePoint tenant is the site. All content added and all work done in SharePoint is done within the context of a site. A SharePoint site collection is a collection of such sites.

Each site collection has a root site, which in turn can contain subsites, pages and apps in the form of lists, libraries and other apps. Each site collection can have all the lower levels, and things like permissions, navigation and themes can be inherited from higher to lower levels.

As each site except the root site of a site collection is created from an existing site, every created site except the site collection root site is a subsite and has a parent site.

The site settings control how the site works and looks. You can reach the settings for the site via the settings in the right part of the Office 365 navigation bar.

6.2.1   The SharePoint Admin Center

In the SharePoint Admin center you can see and manage a lot of settings for the SharePoint part of the Office 365 tenant. To reach the SharePoint Admin center, click on the Admin tile in the Office 365 App Launcher. Now the Office 365 Admin center will open, and at the bottom of the left pane you can find the link to the SharePoint Admin center.

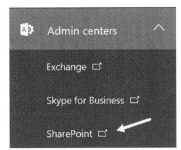

In the SharePoint Admin center, you can see all the tenant's site collections and create new ones. Even the first time you visit the

SharePoint admin center, it has some links to site collections that are created automatically when SharePoint is installed.

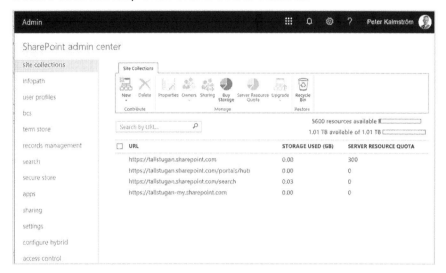

6.2.1.1   Create a New Site Collection

Administrators can create new site collections in the SharePoint Admin center. The new site collection will have a root site and some libraries, see below.

1. Click on the 'New' button in the ribbon and select 'Private Site Collection'. (There used to be the ability to create a public site collection, but that ability is no longer available)

2. A new site collection dialog will open. Give the new site collection a name and select a site template for the root site. The default choice is the classic team site. Make the other settings you prefer, and click OK.

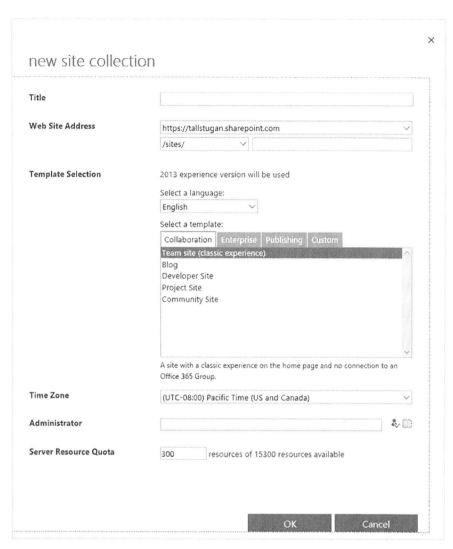

new site collection

Title	
Web Site Address	https://tallstugan.sharepoint.com ∨
	/sites/ ∨
Template Selection	2013 experience version will be used
	Select a language:
	English ∨
	Select a template:
	Collaboration / Enterprise / Publishing / Custom
	Team site (classic experience)
	Blog
	Developer Site
	Project Site
	Community Site
	A site with a classic experience on the home page and no connection to an Office 365 Group.
Time Zone	(UTC-08:00) Pacific Time (US and Canada) ∨
Administrator	
Server Resource Quota	300 resources of 15300 resources available

OK   Cancel

It might take up to 15 minutes for SharePoint to create the new site collection.

In the creation process, SharePoint creates a root site for the site collection, with this URL: https://[tenant].sharepoint.com/sites/[site collection name].

Thus, the site collection created in the image above will have the root site URL https://kalmstromnet.sharepoint.com/sites/Example/

SharePoint also creates the default document libraries, among them the Documents, Site Assets and Site Pages libraries. Your choice of site template decides which default apps are included in the top site of your new site collection and which features are enabled by default. URLs to subsites, pages and apps in this site collection will of course also begin in the same way.

By default, everything in a site collection also share the same permissions, because if you don't break the inheritance, lower levels, like lists/libraries and items/documents, inherit the same permissions as the higher level.

One tenant can have from a few up to 500 000 site collections. I would recommend that you have many, instead of gathering too much data in the same site collection.

Demo:

https://www.kalmstrom.com/Tips/SharePoint-Online-Course/Create-A-New-Site-Collection.htm

6.2.2   Site Contents

To see all the contents of a SharePoint site, open the settings gear in the right part of the Office 365 navigation bar and select 'Site contents'. You can also click on the 'Site Contents' link in the left hand panel, the so called Quick Launch. A page with links to all content will open.

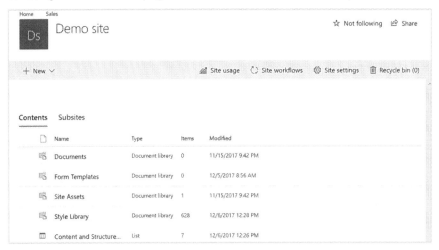

6.2.2.1   Create New

You can create new SharePoint content directly from the Site Contents. Open the '+ New' dropdown in the left part of the command bar and select one of the options.

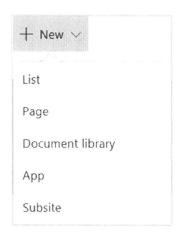

When you select 'List', you will have a blank list app with just a title column. SharePoint will give hints on how you can customize it.

When you select 'Document library', a library with the columns "Name", "Modified" and "Modified By" will be created.

When you select 'App', you will have a choice of app templates for various purposes. Learn more about apps in 6.4 below.

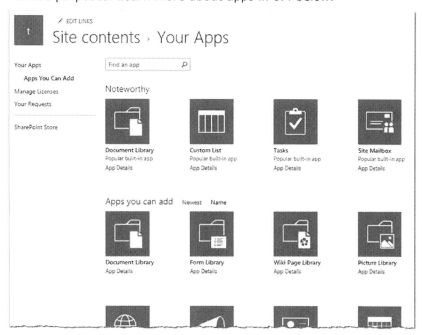

When you select 'Page' a modern page will be created; *refer to* 6.3.2.

When you create a new subsite, there are different kinds of site templates to select from. The Team Site, which is selected by default, is the most commonly used site template, just as when you create a new site collection.

Select a template:

Collaboration | Enterprise | Publishing | Duet Enterprise

Team site (classic experience)
Blog
Project Site
Community Site

A site with a classic experience on the home page and no connection to an Office 365 Group.

By default, subsites inherit permissions and users from the parent site. All users with edit permission on the site (which is default for users) can create subsites.

6.2.3 The Classic Team Site Home Page

The team site is intended for work group collaboration, and it is the most used type of SharePoint site. There are two types of team sites, the classic team site, which we will look at here, and a more limited modern team site which is used with Office 365 Groups; *refer to* chapter 9. (The modern team site can be created from the SharePoint Online home page, *see* 6.5.1.1 below.)

The image below shows the default home page (Home.aspx) of a classic team site. It is a so-called wiki page, and it is intended to be customized to fit each organization. Here we will use the home page to go through the different parts.

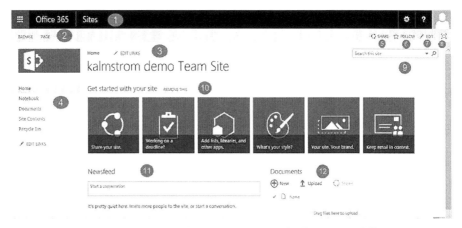

1. The Office 365 section is the same as you find in most Office 365 apps; *refer to* 2.5. There is however an important difference for the SharePoint administrator, because the settings gear has many options for managing and modifying the SharePoint site. Ordinary users with Edit permissions on the site can also add new apps and pages from under that gear.

2. The SharePoint ribbon has various controls under the tabs. As in the Office ribbon, the tabs and controls within those tabs vary depending on what you have selected and which object you are working with. The image below shows the controls under the PAGE tab.

3. The Top Navigation usually shows links to sites within the same site collection.

4. The Quick Launch usually shows links to apps within the current site.

5. The SHARE command is used to share the site.

6. Each user can use the FOLLOW command to follow the site. The user can find all his/her followed sites in the SharePoint Online home page; *refer to* 6.5.

7. The EDIT command opens the page in edit mode, so that you can customize it. When a page is open in edit mode the EDIT command is replaced by a SAVE command.

8. The Focus on Content command shows the page without the navigation parts. Click on the icon again to show the navigation.

9. The Search field is used for global search in SharePoint. By default, the current site is searched, but the search can be filtered or you can search in all content of the tenant.

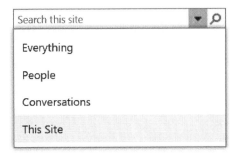

10. The Get Started tiles give links that may be important when you are new to SharePoint. These tiles are often removed after a while, when the team site should be customized. They are easy to remove by clicking on REMOVE THIS.

11. The Newsfeed is intended for sharing information and ideas among the people who use the team site.

12. SharePoint stores different kinds of files in document libraries, but the content of those libraries can also be displayed in a page by using an app part. The home page contains an app part that displays the files that are contained in the default Documents library. Here you can create new files, upload existing files and search among those files.

Demo:

https://www.kalmstrom.com/Tips/Office-365-Course/Start-With-SharePoint.htm

6.3 PAGES

A SharePoint page has a big area in the middle of the SharePoint interface, delimited by the Top navigation menu and the Quick Launch. Each page has its own URL. Here we will have a look at the site pages, which give many customization possibilities.

How a site page looks, depends on how you customize the area in the middle and what content you place there. Site pages can contain text, images, video and web parts (which in turn can display app content).

Site pages are files, and they are stored in a library called Site Pages, which you can find in the Site Contents.

🏶   Site Pages

When you create a new page, you most often create a wiki page or a modern page. Both these are site pages, but they are customized in different ways.

6.3.1 Wiki Pages

The wiki page is the page that gives you the best customization possibilities. The home site of a classic team site, *see* above, is a wiki page.

6.3.1.1 Create a Wiki Page

To create a wiki page, open the Site Pages library under Site Contents. (The 'Site Page' option in the dropdown here refers to the modern page; *see* below.)

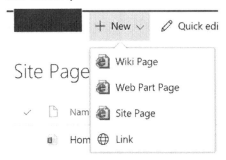

6.3.1.2 Edit a Wiki Page

The new page will open in edit mode, but if you want to modify the wiki page later you can open it in edit mode via the settings gear in the Office 365 navigation bar.

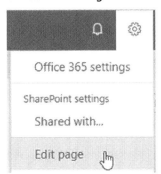

Now you can add text or links or insert images, videos etc. directly into the page or insert various kinds of web parts and customize them.

Demo:

https://www.kalmstrom.com/Tips/SharePoint-Online-Course/Start-Edit-Webpart.htm

6.3.2 Modern Pages

Modern pages are modified with web parts, and they are very easy to customize. But simplicity is in focus, not power and advanced features. Therefore, the modern page does not give as many customization options as the wiki page.

When you create a modern page, there is no name giving. Instead you should change the text in the banner of the newly created page. That text will be used for automatic name giving. (Click on the X in the left toolbar to remove the background image and thereby reduce the big banner area.)

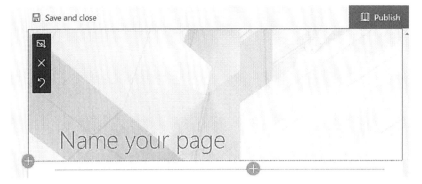

6.3.2.1 Create a Modern Page

A modern page is what you get when you create a new page by clicking on the settings gear and selecting 'Add a page', or by clicking on '+ New' in the Site Contents and selecting 'Page'. You can also select the 'Site Page' option in the Site Pages library; see the image above in 6.3.1.1.

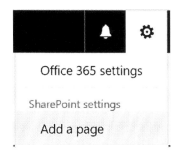

6.3.2.2   Edit a Modern page

The new page will open in edit mode. If you want to modify it later, click on the edit button to the right in the command bar to open a modern page in edit mode.

 Edit

Modern pages can only be customized with specially designed web parts. They can be combined on the page to make it interesting and useful, but each web part can only be modified to a limited extent.

Before you start adding web parts, you should decide how many columns you want to have in the first section. Click on the plus sign to the left to show the choices. One column is default.

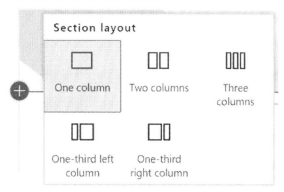

You can have multiple sections below each other with a different number of columns. Just click on the left plus sign again to select a new section layout.

Show the web parts by clicking on the plus sign in the middle of the page or column. Then add the part you prefer to the page by clicking on its icon. After that you can continue and add more web parts beside or below the first one.

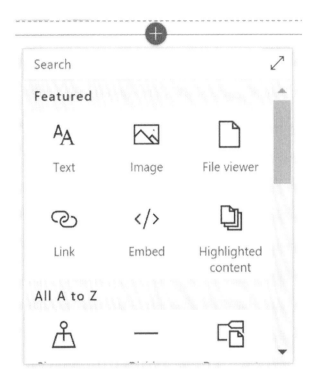

The web parts and sections can be edited or removed via a toolbox to the left of the part/section:

- When you click on the edit icon, you can either start editing directly in the web part, or the web part options will be displayed in a settings pane to the right.
  For sections, you can only change the number of columns.

- Click on the icon in the middle of the toolbox and hold, to drag web parts or sections to new places on the page.

- Click on the basket to remove the part or section.

When you start editing the web part, changes will be saved automatically. When you are finished with the editing, either 'Save and close' to continue working with the page later, or 'Publish' the page.

🖫 Save and close ⋮ 📖 Publish

Here I will give a few examples on how you can use various web parts:

- The **Divider** adds a line that separates sections or web parts.

90

- The **Document library** and the **List** web parts shows the library or list you select (from within the site), so that files and items can be opened directly from the page. The web part has a limited command bar and a few view options, and there are no ellipses.

- In the **Hero** web part, you can add up to five items and use images, text and links to draw attention to each. First select where to fetch the item, and then edit the item by adding text and settings in a right pane.

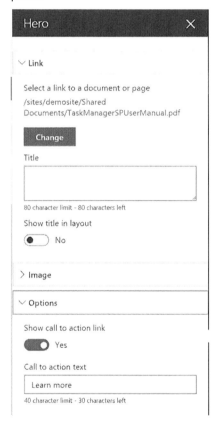

- The **Highlighted content** web part by default searches for and displays the most recently used content, but you can also customize what the web part should search for and display.

- The **News** web part can display a summary of new or existing pages, called News items. When you create a new News item, you are directed to a new modern page. When you are done with creating your page, click on Publish at the top right, and you'll see the story appear in the News section as the most recent story.

- Therefore, the creator of the News web part just adds the part to the page, selects a layout and publishes the part. The actual content comes when you and other users start adding news pages to the web part.

- Recent news posts for the modern page News web part will be displayed on the SharePoint Online home page, and they can also be created from there; *refer to* 6.5.2.

- The **Space**r gives a horizontal space. It is possible to change the size by dragging the bottom line. You can also use the arrow keys.

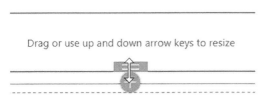

- Several **Office 365 apps** and services have their own modern web parts, where you can display content that has been created with them. Such web parts are Group calendar, Microsoft Forms, Office 365 Stream, Power BI and Yammer. We will look at all those apps later in this book.

Most web parts have names that tell what they can display, and they are not difficult to figure out. Therefore, I will not go more into each of them here, but should you need assistance Microsoft has a good online guide where each modern web part is described in detail:
https://support.office.com/en-us/article/Using-web-parts-on-SharePoint-Online-pages-336e8e92-3e2d-4298-ae01-d404bbe751e0

6.3.2.3   Make a Modern Page the Home Page

A new team site automatically gets a wiki home page, but you can replace it with another page. This is done easily when you use the **modern** interface in the Site pages library (*see* below for modern and classic app interfaces):

1. Open the Site Contents and find 'Site pages' in the list.

2. Open the Site pages library.

3. (Exit the classic experience if necessary.)

4. Select the page you want to set as the site's homepage.

5. Click on the ellipsis in the command bar or at the page and select 'Make homepage'.

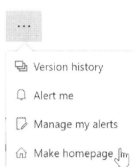

🗗 Version history

🔔 Alert me

🗒 Manage my alerts

🏠 Make homepage 👆

6.3.2.4   Comments

By default, the modern page has a Comments section at the bottom. It can be removed when the page is in edit mode by clicking on the switch button.

Comments 🔘 On

6.3.2.4.1   *Disable Comments*

When a modern page is made into a homepage, the comments section will be disabled automatically on that page.

Administrators can disable the comments section for all modern pages. This is done under SharePoint Admin center >settings. You can find 'Comments on Site pages' at the very bottom.

Demos:

https://www.kalmstrom.com/Tips/SharePoint-Online-Course/New-Page-Model-Intro.htm

https://www.kalmstrom.com/Tips/SharePoint-Online-Course/New-Page-Model-Text.htm

https://www.kalmstrom.com/Tips/SharePoint-Online-Course/New-Page-Model-Highlighted.htm

6.4   APPS

Within SharePoint sites, content can be stored and shared in apps. Document libraries, picture libraries, contact lists and calendars are all examples on apps, and all app types have common features.

SharePoint apps can be of three different types:

- Lists. A list is very much like a database or Excel table. It contains items such as appointments in a calendar list, contacts in a contact list or tasks in a tasks list. You can also create your own custom list such as a Cost Center list. Each list has many settings, for example which columns, views and permissions should be used on that list. (Note that items can contain attached files, but the main objects in a list are the items, not the files.)

- Document libraries. A library can do almost everything that a list can do and it has most of the same settings and features. The main difference is that libraries contain files instead of items. Each "row" in a document library represents a single file, which has built-in properties (column values), such as 'Created' and 'Modified By', and custom properties, for example 'Cost Center'.

- Apps that are purchased or built by your organization and added to SharePoint. Such apps are often called Add-ins.

A SharePoint app is similar to a database table or spreadsheet. Data is distributed in rows, and each row is known as an item. Each row, or item, has various columns where you enter metadata that describes the item.

SharePoint apps have many benefits:

- SharePoint apps give a good overview over data.

- Use the powerful SharePoint Search to find information.

- The version history feature lets you see earlier versions of each item and what exactly was changed in each version. Version history is enabled by default in most document libraries but disabled by default in most lists.

- You can filter and sort items to study the information in different ways.

- You can create different views to permanently filter or display items in a particular way.

- With the Totals feature you can summarize values from your items with sum, average etc. (Currently only in the classic experience.)

- You can connect and export SharePoint data to Excel. In the classic experience you can also connect and export to Outlook, Access, Visio and Project.

- You can set permissions on a singular item or folder, so that only some people can view or edit it.

- You can let SharePoint send alerts when items have been added, changed or deleted.

6.4.1 Modern and Classic Experiences

Many apps are available in two user interfaces: the classic and the modern experience. The modern interface is better adapted to smart devices and more touch friendly than the classic one.

Most apps can be viewed in both the classic and the modern interface. Below are images from the upper part of two document libraries, and I hope they will give an idea about the differences between the two experiences.

Classic:

Modern:

The modern experience is more intuitive to use, so it is easier to manage for the average user. However, some things can only be done with the classic interface. On the other hand, there are modern features that do not exist in the classic experience also, for example direct connections to Flow and PowerApps; *refer to* chapter 14.

Even if most apps can be viewed in both interfaces, some, like the calendar, contacts and tasks lists, still only have the classic interface.

When apps can be viewed in both interfaces, they have links in the bottom left corner: 'Return to classic SharePoint' in the modern experience and 'Exit classic experience' in the classic interface.

Return to classic SharePoint

Exit classic experience

Microsoft is not deprecating the classic experience. Instead the classic and modern interfaces will coexist. Administrators need to learn both the modern and the classic SharePoint experience and be able to judge which interface is best for each purpose.

Note that it is the same app whether you use the modern or classic experience. If you make a change in the app contents or settings and then switch interface, you will see the change in the other interface also.

(Compare the two app interfaces with modern and classic team sites and pages. Modern team sites and pages can ***not*** be viewed in a classic interface and vice versa. These are different sites and pages, and the interfaces cannot be changed.)

6.4.1.1   Default App Interface

SharePoint administrators can set the default interface for lists and libraries under 'settings' in the SharePoint Admin center, and app owners and administrators can set default experience for each app in its list or library settings >Advanced settings.

These settings does not stop users from switching interface with the links. They just decide what interface is displayed by default.

Demo:

https://www.kalmstrom.com/Tips/SharePoint-Online-Course/Library-Interface.htm

6.4.2   App Settings

Each app has a settings page where you can find many kinds of settings, including settings for permissions, columns and views.

You can reach the settings for all app types from the Site Contents. Click on the ellipsis to the right of the app and select Settings.

When you have the app open, the **modern** interface has a List/Library settings link under the Settings gear.

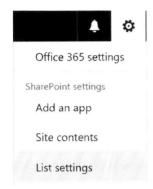

The **classic** interface has the settings link in the ribbon:

- In most lists, the List Settings button is found under the LIST tab in the ribbon.

- In calendars, the List Settings button is found under the CALENDAR tab in the ribbon.

List Settings

- In document libraries, you can find the Library Settings button under the LIBRARY tab in the ribbon.

6.4.3   Document Libraries

Document libraries are often the best way to share documents within an organization, and it is certainly much better than sending e-mail attachments. When you use SharePoint document libraries for file sharing you have everything in one place, and all who have been given permission can reach the library.

I would recommend that you use several document libraries, as a way of categorizing files. For example, if your site is made for sharing information about a new product you could have these libraries:

- Suggested Specifications

- Supplier Contracts

- Design Sketches

- Radio Commercials in .mp3 format

Within these libraries you would of course have files. Those files are sometimes referred to as documents in the SharePoint user interface. You can download files from the document library to your computer and vice versa.

You can add content to a SharePoint library either by creating a new document in SharePoint or by uploading an existing file to the library. The upload of existing files can be done in several different ways.

6.4.3.1   Create a File in a Library

The best way to get content into a SharePoint library, is to create it in SharePoint directly. Click on the '+ New' button in the command bar or above the list of files, to start creating. By default, you will have a choice of creating an Office file or a folder, and in the modern experience you can also add a link to the library.

Follow these steps to create a new file in a SharePoint library:

1. Open the library where you want to create the new file and click on the +New button.

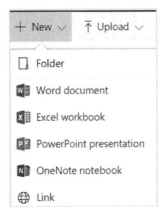

2. A new document will open in edit mode, by default in the online version of the document type you selected. Also *refer to* 4.1.1.3.

Demo:

https://kalmstrom.com/Tips/SharePoint-Online-Course/Create-Content-in-SharePoint.htm

6.4.3.2   Upload Files

Most file types can be uploaded to SharePoint libraries. When you add files to SharePoint by the methods described below, they will be copied to the library. They will not be removed from your PC.

6.4.3.2.1   *Upload Button*

In the **modern** experience, click on the 'Upload' button in the command bar to upload one or several files to a SharePoint library. Here you can also upload a folder.

Select 'Files' or 'Folder'. Then you can browse to the item(s) on your PC that you want to upload and click OK. Now the file will be uploaded.

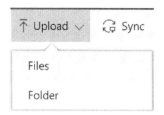

In the **classic** experience, you can either click on the 'Upload' button or on the 'Upload Document' button under the 'FILES' tab in the ribbon.

To select multiple files:

- To select some files, hold down the Ctrl key and click on the files you want to add.

- To select files that are sorted together, hold down the Shift key while you click on the first file and then the last file.

- To select all files in a folder, hold down the Ctrl key and press the A key.

6.4.3.2.2   *Save As*

Another way to upload Office files is to save them directly into a SharePoint library:

1. Copy the path to the SharePoint library from the address field in your browser. Leave out the last part, which should look like this: Forms/AllItems.aspx.

2. In the open document, click on 'Save as' under the 'File' tab.

3. Click on 'Browse'.

4. Paste the path you copied into the address field.

5. Click on the arrow to the right of the address field, or press Enter.

6. (You have to log in to SharePoint, if you have not saved your log in information.)

7. Click on Save.

In section 8.3 below, I have described another way to move files to a SharePoint library: synchronize a library with a folder in Windows Explorer.

Demo:

https://kalmstrom.com/Tips/SharePoint-Online-Course/Upload-File.htm

6.4.3.2.3 *Drag and Drop*

If you have a modern browser, you can drag and drop files from your PC to a SharePoint Online library. This can be done with one file or with multiple files at the same time, so drag and drop is a fast and convenient way to add files to SharePoint document libraries.

1. Open Windows Explorer on your PC in a small window over the SharePoint library window, or put the two windows side by side using the Windows button + the left/right keys.

2. Select the file(s) you want to copy to the library.

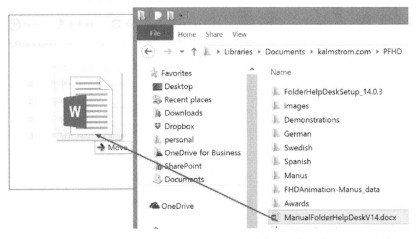

3. Drag the files to the box that becomes visible in the library and drop them there.

You may also keep the Windows Explorer window maximized and drag the files to the browser icon. The browser will then open in the latest visited window, and if that is the SharePoint library you can drop the file as described in point 3 above.

Demo:

https://www.kalmstrom.com/Tips/SharePoint-Online-Course/Upload-Multiple-Files-Drag.htm

6.4.3.3 Sync files

It is possible to have SharePoint libraries as folders in Windows Explorer on a PC or smart device and synchronize files between those folders and the libraries.

When you have such a library folder in your PC, it is convenient to just drag or copy and paste files from other folders to the library folder. They will be uploaded automatically when you are online and connected to Office 365. *Refer to* 8.3 for more information about this synchronization.

6.5 THE SHAREPOINT ONLINE HOME PAGE

When a user clicks on the SharePoint tile in the Office 365 App Launcher, he/she is directed to the SharePoint Online home page.

The SharePoint Online home page is a kind of SharePoint Favorites page. Here each SharePoint user can find links to SharePoint sites he or she has decided to follow, to recent or frequently used sites, to news and to sites promoted by the organization.

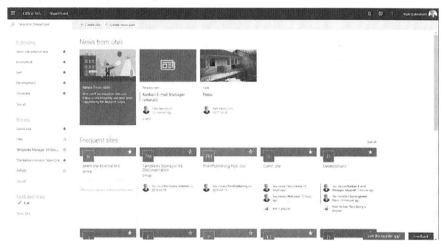

Here I will focus on the two buttons right below the Office 365 navigation bar.

＋ Create site   ＋ Create news post

6.5.1 Create Site

A new team site can be created in several ways. I explained how to create a subsite in 6.2.2.1, and most often such a subsite is based on the classic team site template. You can also create a new site collection built on any site template from the SharePoint Admin Center.

In this section, I will describe how users can create new, limited, team sites or communication sites to manage projects and related documents and communications. This is done from the 'Create site' button on the SharePoint Online home page.

Administrators can limit or disable this possibility, *refer to* 6.5.1.4 below.

The sites created from the SharePoint home page are modern sites with some limitations compared to regular sites. Their home pages are modern, *refer to* 6.3.2 above, and can only be customized with dedicated web parts, which you can add, remove or reorder as needed. You can also add new apps, pages and even classic subsites to these sites.

The new site will appear among the user's followed sites. It will not inherit permission settings or navigation of other sites, as it is a totally new site collection.

(If the site should inherit permissions or navigation and be connected to other sites, it is better to create it as a subsite in an existing site collection, *refer to* 6.2.2.1.)

The first creation steps are the same for the two site types.

1. Click on the 'Create site' button to the right of the Search box in the Favorites page.

2. Select the site type you want to use. The team site is meant for collaboration on a specific project and the communication site for showing information to a broader audience.

Create a site
Choose the type of site you'd like to create

Team site
Share documents, have conversations with your team, keep track of events, manage tasks, and more with a site connected to an Office 365 group.

Communication site
Publish dynamic, beautiful content to people in your organization to keep them informed and engaged on topics, events, or projects.

3. Give the site a name and a description.

6.5.1.1   Team Site

When you select to create a team site, an Office 365 Group will be created automatically, and all users added to the site will be members of that group. Therefore, the modern team site is also called "group site".

The group will have a shared e-mail inbox, and the group e-mail name will by default be the same as the team site name. *Refer to* chapter 9 for more info about Office 365 Groups.

Follow these steps to continue the creation of a team site.

1. Add a description and decide if the team site (and the group) should be public (so that anyone in the organization can access it) or private.

2. Click on Next.

3. Add group members. If the group is private, only these people will have access to the site. You will automatically be the owner of the team site, but you can add additional owners. Also *refer to* Permissions below.

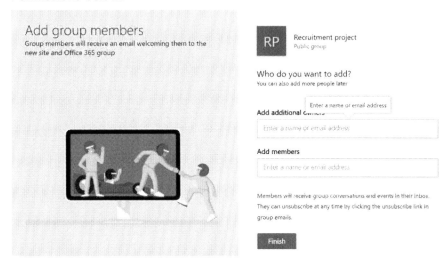

4. Click on Finish.

Now the new site will open. By default, the home page has four web parts, News, Quick Links, Activity and Documents, but you can customize it and create apps and pages if needed.

All members you added will receive an e-mail where they are welcomed to the site, and they can see group conversations and events in their work mailbox.

(Another way to create the modern team site that is described here, is to first create an Office 365 Group from Office 365 Outlook; *refer to* chapter 9. A modern team site will then be created automatically.)

6.5.1.1.1 *Permissions*

To see and change the permissions on a group site, click on the settings gear in the right part of the Office 365 navigation bar and select 'Site permissions'.

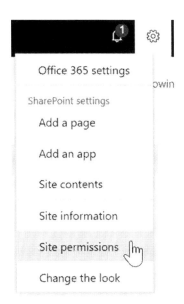

A right pane with permission options will open. The image below shows the default permissions. As you see all members you have added – and for public groups everyone else in the organization too! – have Edit permission. You can change that into Read, if the information is sensitive. Your changes are saved automatically when you click outside the pane.

Site permissions

To view or change the group members for this site, go to Outlook.

∧ Full Control

  Group owners

∧ Edit

  Everyone except external users
Edit ∨

  Group members
Edit ∨

∧ Read

6.5.1.2   Communication site

When you select to create a Communication site, you will have three different templates to choose from.

Select 'Topic' to share information such as news, events, and other content. Select 'Showcase' to showcase a product, team or event with photos or images. When you choose 'Blank' you will start with an empty modern home page.

The image below shows the default template, Topic.

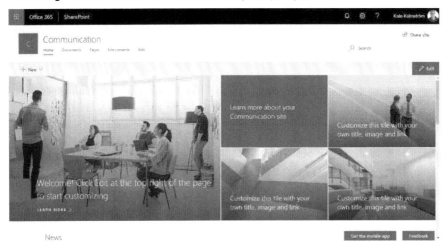

No group is created with the communication site, so you should use the 'Share site' icon in the top right corner to invite people to the site.

The communication sites have no Quick Launch. Instead, the local navigation is found on top, where you find the global navigation in classic team sites. This theme is called "Oslo".

6.5.1.3   Differences

The image below gives a summary of the differences between the two modern sites and the classic team site.

Feature	Communication Site	Group Team Site	Classic Team Site
Solutions gallery			X
Save as template			X
Manage through SP Admin center			X
Oslo theme	X		
Modern first page	X	X	
Office 365 Group		X	
Created by any user	X	X	
Default external sharing		X	

6.5.1.4   Site Creation Admin Control

The 'Create site' option is enabled by default, but administrators can disable and control the feature in the SharePoint Admin center.

Under 'settings', make your choices in the 'Site Creation' section.

The team and communication sites form their own site collections, but they do not show up in the SharePoint Admin center list of site collections. For team sites, the admin can manage the groups in the Office 365 admin center, but when this is written, Microsoft has not given administrators a way to see the communication sites.

Demo:

https://kalmstrom.com/Tips/SharePoint-Online-Course/3-site-collections.htm

6.5.2 Create News Post

When you click on the 'Create news post' button in the SharePoint home page, a right pane will open where you can select where the news post should be published.

When you have selected the site, a new modern page will open. Give it a title and add your news item, *refer to* 6.3.2.2.

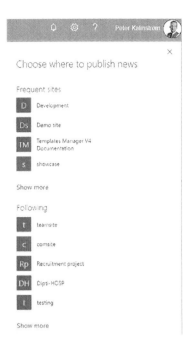

6.6 SUMMARY

In this chapter, I have given a short explanation on what SharePoint is used for and what content SharePoint sites can have. You have also learned how to reach the SharePoint Admin center, how to create a new site collections, sites, pages and apps and how to see the contents and settings of a site and app.

Finally I have described how users can create modern sites and news pages from the SharePoint Online home page. Make sure you have noted that there are two team site types: the classic team site and the modern group team site.

For more information about SharePoint Online, refer to my book *SharePoint Online from Scratch.* I have also published a book with step by step instructions on how to build useful solutions to common business scenarios: *SharePoint Online Exercises*. Both are available as e-book and paper-back on Amazon.

In the next chapters we will have a look at Delve and OneDrive for Business, which both build on SharePoint. We will also come back to SharePoint later, when we look into Office 365 Groups and the site and apps that are created for each new group.

7   DELVE

When users click on the Delve icon, they will be directed to https://delve.office.com/, a site where they can create and show a personal profile to the organization. Delve can be much personalized, and used in the right way it can be very informative and even fun.

The details given in Delve will help people within the organization to get to know each other, and both employees and managers can find people with special interest or expertise. This will of course benefit the organization as well as the individual.

Each user has his/her own content in Delve, but note that Delve never changes any permissions. Users will only see what they are allowed to see.

7.1   OFFICE GRAPH

In Delve users can see, open and manage information that is relevant to them. The Office Graph, which continuously collects and analyses data about working habits in Office 365, decides what should be displayed, but users can group the documents and add them to their favorites.

The Office Graph is enabled by default, but administrators can disable it in the SharePoint Admin center >settings >Office Graph.

If you don't allow access to the Office Graph, you will disable Delve functionality and also affect content that is displayed elsewhere in Office 365, like in the SharePoint home page and in the OneDrive for Business Discover view.

7.2   DELVE HOME

When you select Delve in the Office 365 App Launcher or open delve.office.com in the browser you will reach the Delve home page. Here Delve wants to help users find the information that is most interesting to them. Therefore the main area in the Delve home page has cards with file info. (The left pane is described below.)

Delve can find files when they are stored and shared in OneDrive for Business (*see* chapter 8) or SharePoint Online. Videos from Office 365 Stream (*see* chapter 11) and links from Yammer (*see* chapter 15) can also show up in the Delve home page. For new users the page may be empty, like in the image below.

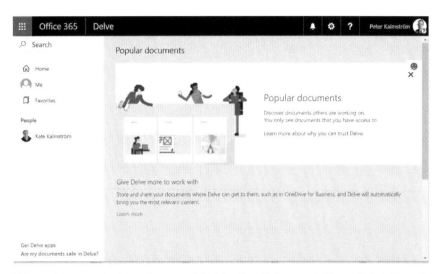

When documents have been added to OneDrive and SharePoint libraries, they will begin to fill up the Delve home page. The user's most recent files are displayed together with files that the user's contacts have been working with – if the user has access to them, of course.

7.2.1   Document cards

Delve shows document cards on several pages. You can open the document by clicking on the card, but each card also gives a lot of information about the file it represents.

a. The author/creator of the file.

b. The modified date. Year is displayed if it is an earlier year.

c. A preview of the document.

d. The file type.

e. The file name.

f. The name of the library where the file is stored.

g. The file's number of views.

h. A Favorite icon. The file in the image above is marked as a Favorite, so it can also be found on the Delve Favorites page.

i. A Board icon. The file in the image above is added to a board, where it is the only file so far. The user can reach his/her boards from the left pane.

j. An ellipsis that gives more choices. The Yammer option opens a right pane with a Yammer conversation; *refer to* 12.2.13.

7.3 DELVE LEFT PANE

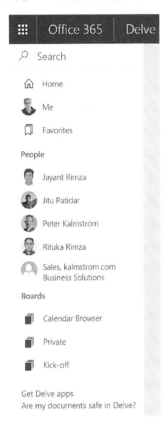

The Delve left pane is always the same. It has a search box and links to the 'Home', 'Me' and 'Favorites' pages.

Colleagues relevant to the user are shown under 'People', and when you click on a contact you can see the personal information this colleague has shared. You can of course also use the search to find someone that is not present in the Delve left pane.

You can also click on a person's name or picture anywhere in Delve to go to their profile page.

Documents displayed in Delve can be grouped in Boards, and the names of these boards are also shown in the left pane.

There are Delve apps for the most common phones and tablets, downloadable from the app stores via a link in the left pane.

Finally the Delve left pane has a link to security information by Microsoft.

7.4 DELVE 'ME' PAGE

If you enter Delve by clicking on 'My profile' under the user icon/photo in the top right corner of all Office 365 pages, you will directly reach the Delve 'Me' page.

Recent documents are displayed here, as well as on the home page, but the main purpose of the 'Me' page is to be a source of information about the user.

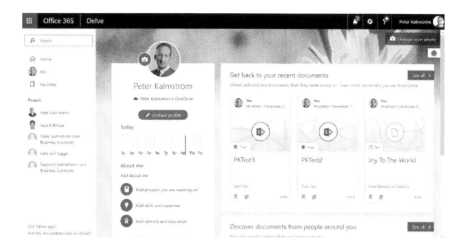

Users can share contact information, projects and interests and announce any speciality under 'Ask me about'. They can even have their own blog.

Below the profile picture, Delve has an overview over today's schedule and a link to the default OneDrive for Business library.

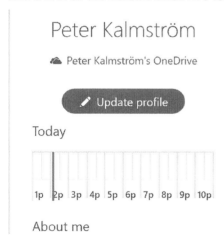

There is also an 'Update profile' button, which links to a page with sections for contact details, interests, schools, expertise and more. Some of these sections also have their own links below the schedule.

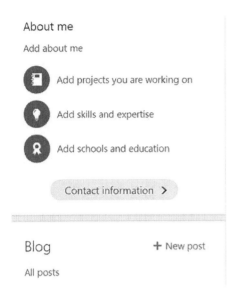

7.4.1 Profile Picture

Microsoft has intended for each Office 365 user to show a photo. The image is added to the account and shown in various ways throughout Office 365 to identify users and help people recognize each other.

7.4.1.1 Size and Resolution

You can use any image for the profile photo, but for best result it should be square and if possible of the size 283x283 pixels. I recommend a resolution of 240 PPI.

In most cases a photo with a white background works best. Office 365 does not support a transparent background.

7.4.1.2 Upload a Profile Picture

The default picture in Office 365 is either a stylized human figure or a circle with your initials. When the account is new and there is still no photo added to it, you can click on the profile picture icon and then on 'Change' to add a photo.

Now you can upload a photo and save it – or delete it and try with another photo.

The icons will be replaced with your photo, but the links, 'Change' and 'Upload' will still be there in case you want to change the photo.

7.4.1.3 Change Profile Picture

There are two ways to change the profile picture.

- Click on your profile picture in the right corner of each Office 365 page to see options. Then click on the picture again, and a window where you can upload a new photo will open.

- Click on 'My profile under your profile picture in the right corner of each Office 365 page. This will take you to Delve. In the Delve home page, click on the camera icon at the photo above your name.

Demo:

https://www.kalmstrom.com/Tips/Office-365-Course/Profile-Picture.htm

7.5 SUMMARY

Microsoft has made an effort to help colleagues within an organization to get to know each other and learn what skills each person has. Of course, the users must also make an effort and really use these possibilities by giving relevant information. In this chapter you have learned how you can introduce yourself to your colleagues with the help of Delve and how you can manage the files displayed there.

8 ONEDRIVE FOR BUSINESS

With OneDrive for Business, which is included in all Office 365 business subscriptions, users can store files in the cloud, synchronize them with their desktop or smart devices and share them with others. The default OneDrive for Business URL is https://TENANT-my.sharepoint.com.

OneDrive for Business gives each user a site collection with 1 TB storage space, and in the E3 and E5 subscriptions the storage space is even unlimited.

In this chapter I will describe how you can share files that are stored in a OneDrive library and how the synchronization is set up between OneDrive and other SharePoint libraries on one side and folders in your PC on the other side.

I will also explain how you can take advantage of the OneDrive for Business site collection to make yourself the administrator of your own SharePoint site collection.

(There is also a "OneDrive" included in Windows 8.1 and 10. It is connected to your Microsoft account – not to your organizational Office 365 account. It has less storage space and does not build on a SharePoint site collection, and that "OneDrive" is *not* what we are talking about here.)

8.1 THE FILES LIBRARY

When you click on the OneDrive tile in the Office 365 App Launcher or at office.com, you will reach the default library in the OneDrive site collection, 'Files'. This library has a special design and is easy to use, but it also has limitations compared to other SharePoint libraries.

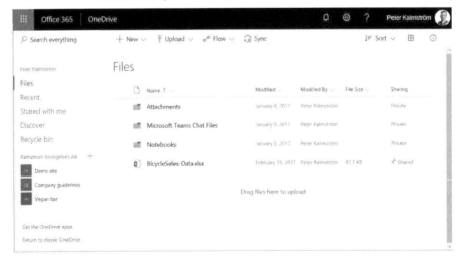

You can share files and folders in the 'Files' library and add new content to it in the same way as with all SharePoint libraries. However, the OneDrive 'Files' library lacks many other library features.

Because of these limitations, I often recommend users to create new libraries in OneDrive instead of using the 'Files' library, *refer to* 8.3.2 below. These new libraries will have the standard SharePoint library features.

8.1.1   Office 365 Group

You can create a new Office 365 Group with a modern team site from the OneDrive for Business Files library. This is the same kind of team site and Office 365 Group as you can create from the SharePoint home page; *refer to* 6.5.1.1. Click on the plus sign in the left pane to get started.

8.2   SHARE ONEDRIVE FILES

All files that you store in OneDrive for Business are private until you decide to share them, which is an important difference to standard SharePoint libraries.

You can easily share files with different groups of people in your organization by placing them in special 'Shared' folders. You can also share just one file or folder with specified colleagues.

Select the file or folder you want to share and click on the 'Share' icon or the 'Share' command under the ellipsis. You can also use the 'Share' button in the command bar.

A dialog will open where you can enter people you want to share with. If they are within the tenant, you will have suggestions when you start writing.

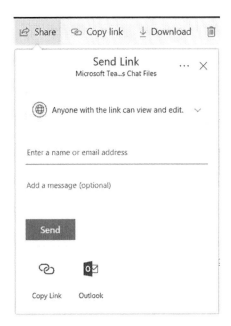

Here you can also get a link to the item you want to share. The Outlook option opens an e-mail with a link.

I strongly recommend you to open the dropdown at "Anyone with the link can view and edit." Then you will have more options for the sharing.

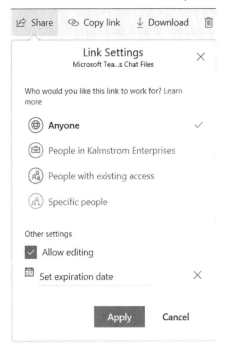

As you see in the image above, *edit* is the default permission when you share OneDrive files or folders. Uncheck the 'Allow editing' box, if you want to only allow the people you share with to view the file.

Here you can also restrict the sharing in other ways, for example set an expiration date.

8.2.1 E-mail Links

When you click on the 'Attach' button in an e-mail in a mailbox that is open in Outlook Web App, the default option is to attach a OneDrive for Business file as a link, instead of sending it as an attachment.

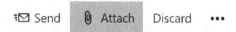

This saves mailbox space, and people can edit the same copy of a file in OneDrive for Business; *refer to* 4.1.1.4. But it also has a disadvantage: By sending a link to a file in your OneDrive for Business library, you automatically give the receiver(s) permission to edit the file.

Therefore, you should always be aware that you allow editing when you send such links. If you want people to just be able to read the file, share it from the OneDrive site instead and change the default permission by unchecking the 'Allow editing' box, as described above.

Demo:

https://www.kalmstrom.com/Tips/SharePoint-Online-Course/OneDrive-Intro.htm

8.3   SYNC BETWEEN ONEDRIVE AND PC FOLDER

Each Office 365 user can add his/her Files library as a folder in a personal computer or smart device and edit the files there.

Other SharePoint libraries can also be synchronized to the PC in the same way as described below, but there is no choice on what to sync, as described in point 4 in the section below. When you sync another library than the Files library, everything in the library will be synced.

Once the synchronization is set up, the files are synchronized automatically when the user is logged in to Office 365, and there is also a manual synchronization.

8.3.1 Manual Sync

Once you have set up the synchronization between the Files library and your PC or smart device, OneDrive for Business will keep track of changes and synchronize the library and folder automatically. However, the first time you must ⟳ Sync do it manually. You can also perform the steps below anytime if you need to make a manual sync.

1. Open the Files library and click on the 'Sync' button in the command bar.

2. A 'Getting ready to sync' dialog will open. It has a link to download OneDrive for Business, but if you have already installed the Office 365 ProPlus package, *refer to* 4.1.1., you should not download anything.

3. You might be asked to open OneDrive for Business and/or to log in with your Office 365 account.

4. Another dialog will open. By default all files and folders in the library are synchronized, but you can uncheck that option and instead check only those that you want to sync. (If you don't see this dialog, look for the OneDrive icon in the task bar and click on it to open the dialog.)

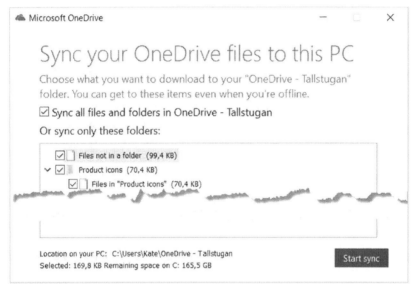

5. Click on the 'Start sync' button.

6. If this is the first time you synchronize the Files library, OneDrive for Business creates a new folder on your device. It has the name OneDrive-TENANT, and you can see the path to it in the dialog where you select what to sync. It is not possible to sync to another folder.

7. All the files in the Files library that you selected to sync are now shown in the new folder. From now on, OneDrive for Business will keep track of changes and synchronize this library and folder automatically.

If you add the new OneDrive folder to your Favorites/Quick access, it will be smooth to move files between that folder and your other folders. When you drag or copy/cut and paste items to the OneDrive folder, they will be automatically uploaded to the Files library when you are online and logged into Office 365.

8.3.1.1   Sync Limitations

If the synchronization does not work, you can consider if one of these points can be the problem.

- The file is open.

- The file or folder name has a character that is not supported: \, /, :, *, ?, ", <, >, | , # , %,~.

- The SharePoint library has more than 5000 items.

8.3.1.2   Sync Settings

Right click on the OneDrive icon in the task bar to reach the OneDrive for Business settings. Here you can stop synchronizing, pause the syncing, change the folders to sync, perform a manual sync and more.

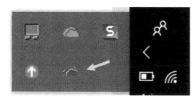

(You might need to click on the 'Show hidden icons' arrow to see the OneDrive icon.)

8.3.2   Selective Synchronization

One way of taking advantage of your personal site collection is to create new libraries for your own use or for sharing. This gives important advantages and lets you synchronize in a more controlled way than if you only use the default OneDrive for Business library.

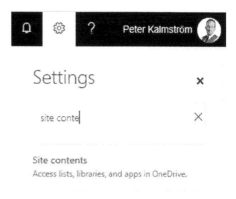

The Files library does not show the Site Contents, so you have to open the settings gear and search for it. Then you can create new libraries as described in 6.2.2.1.

The synchronization of other SharePoint libraries works in the same way as with the default OneDrive library, *see* above.

When you synchronize another SharePoint library for the first time, OneDrive for Business creates a new folder on your PC with the name of the tenant. All libraries that you synchronize will be added as subfolders under the folder with the tenant name.

Creating new SharePoint libraries has important benefits:

- SharePoint does not work well when you have more than 5000 files in a library. If you create more libraries in the OneDrive site collection, you will overcome that problem and still have unlimited storage.

- When you create several libraries, you can choose to not synchronize all of them to your device. The libraries you don't synchronize, can be used for storage of files you don't need to access very often. You can also sync different libraries with different devices.

Note that the new library folders will show up as a subfolder under a folder with your tenant name on your PC.

The 'OneDrive + tenant' name folder only contains the default OneDrive for Business library. The tenant name in the image to the right is "Tallstugan".

 Tallstugan

 OneDrive - Tallstugan

Demos:

https://www.kalmstrom.com/Tips/SharePoint-Online-Course/OneDrive-Sync.htm

https://kalmstrom.com/Tips/SharePoint-Online-Course/OneDrive-More-Libraries.htm

8.4 SUMMARY

OneDrive for Business gives Office 365 user a personal site collection and a possibility to share and synchronize files and folders. We have looked at the default OneDrive for Business document library, and you should now understand how you can share files from that library and what to think about when you do it.

We have also looked at the synchronization feature that is present in all SharePoint libraries and managed by OneDrive for Business, and I have explained how to find the OneDrive Site Contents and create new apps in your personal site collection.

9 OFFICE 365 GROUPS

In an Office 365 Group, users can share documents, work on project plans together, schedule meetings and receive e-mails in a shared inbox – often concerning a specific topic, such as a project.

The Groups service is supported in all Office 365 subscriptions that include Exchange and SharePoint, and it is intended to be an extended and more user friendly replacement for the earlier distribution lists and shared mailboxes.

Office 365 Groups are used in several Office 365 apps, and when changes to group content or membership is made in one app it may take a few minutes before it shows up in another app.

9.1 GROUP CREATION METHODS

An Office 365 Group can be created in several ways. We have already looked at the modern team site, where you first create a modern SharePoint team site and then add people to the Office 365 Group that is created automatically; *refer to* 6.5.1.1 and 8.1.1.

You can also start creating an Office 365 Group from Outlook, and later in this chapter I will describe that method.

Furthermore, Office 365 Groups are created automatically when you create a Planner plan, a Stream group, a Teams team or a StaffHub team; *refer to* chapters 10, 11, 12 and 13.

All Office 365 Resources are not displayed in the app when you start creating an Office 365 group from another app, but they are often possible to add and available from each user's mailbox.

However you start creating the Office 365 Group, the service will quickly set up a collection of resources for the group to share. You don't have to worry about manually creating or assigning permissions to the shared resources, because when you add members to the group, they will automatically get the permissions they need to the tools your group provides.

9.1.1 Admin Restrictions

By default all users can create Office 365 Groups, but administrators can restrict the permission using Azure AD PowerShell, *refer to* https://support.office.com/en-us/article/Manage-Office-365-Group-Creation-4c46c8cb-17d0-44b5-9776-005fced8e618?ui=en-US&rs=en-US&ad=US.

Users who are not allowed to create groups can neither create plans in Planner, Stream groups or teams in Teams. It is still possible to create a StaffHub team, but files and e-mails cannot be shared.

9.2 SEE GROUPS

An Office 365 Group has no interface of its own. Instead, all the Office 365 Groups that a user belongs to are shown in the Folders view of that users Outlook – both in the web app and in the desktop app. From there, users can also join new groups.

Click on 'Folders' if you cannot see the groups.

Click on 'More' to go back again.

Office 365 Groups are also visible in other places, in apps where they are used.

9.3 JOIN A GROUP

Office 365 Groups support over 1000 members, but I recommend you to have much smaller groups. Accessing group conversations and the group calendar may take long with several hundreds of users.

Users can join public Office 365 Groups spontaneously, but for private groups an invitation is needed. The privacy level is set by the group creator.

9.3.1 Spontaneous Joining

When a new *public* group has been created, it will show up in each user's Outlook, under Groups. Below icons for the groups the user already has joined, there is an arrow and a 'Discover' link that opens a pane with all existing public groups that the user has not yet joined.

The dialog shows who created the group and a group description. Now the user can either 'Go to group', to have a closer look at what the group is intended for, or directly join the group by clicking on the 'Join' button.

9.3.2   Joining after Invitation

When a group owner adds a user to an Office 365 Group, that group will show up in his/her Outlook under Groups, and a welcoming e-mail will be sent to the user's inbox. Such additions *can* be made for public groups, and they *must* be done for private groups and for guests (people from outside the tenant).

The subject of the e-mail mentions the inviter:

Kate Kalmström added you to the Marketing group

The e-mail body shows what you can do by joining the group:

The new Marketing group is ready

Marketing;

 Marketing
Fri 2018-02-16 15:03

Welcome to the Marketing group.

Use the group to share ideas, files, and important dates.

Start a conversation

Read group conversations or
start your own.

Add to the team site

Start sharing and collaborating
on content in SharePoint.

Share files

View, edit, and share all group
files, including email
attachments.

Connect your apps

Connect apps like Twitter and
Trello to stay current with
information and updates your
team cares about.

Get the Groups app on your phone and stay connected.

All users can send a link with a joining request to colleagues, but these requests have to be approved by the group owner before the new group member is allowed to join.

Here you can reach the group apps, *refer to* 9.5, and get the group's e-mail address and links to the files library and site by right clicking. You will also have links to Group apps for smart devices.

9.4   CREATE A GROUP FROM OUTLOOK

Here we will show how to create an Office 365 Group from Outlook. In the other apps that use the Groups service, a group is created automatically when a new site, plan, team and so on is created. This is described in the chapters about each app. For an example earlier in this book, *refer to* 6.5.1.1.

In Outlook Web App, click on the plus sign at the Groups folder list to create a new group.

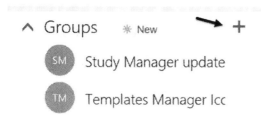

A pane will open to the right, and here you can give the group a name, an e-mail ID and a description and set its privacy level, language and message options.

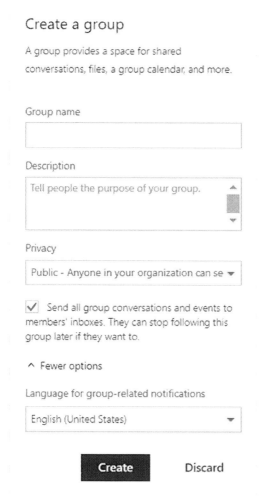

In the desktop edition of Outlook, click on the 'New Group' button in the Group ribbon to create a group.

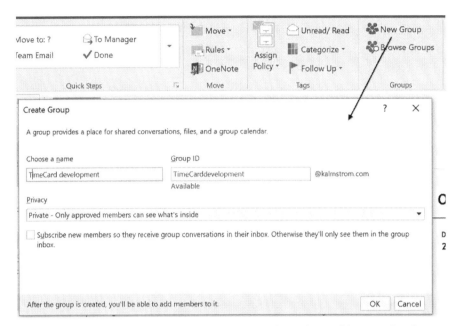

You can also use the 'New Items' button in the Inbox ribbon and select 'Group'.

9.5   GROUP RESOURCES

When you create an Office 365 Group, several shared apps will be created for the group members automatically, and all members will have access to them. Group members can reach these apps from their own Outlook mailboxes, when they select a group they have joined.

Outlook Web App users just have to click on the group entry and then select an app from the command bar. 'Conversations' (default) and 'Files' will open below the command bar, and 'Calendar' will open the OWA calendar view. 'Notebook', 'Planner' and 'Site' will direct the user to new sites, that will open in a new tab.

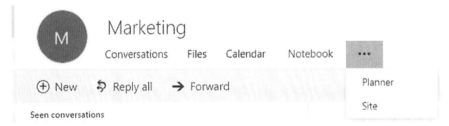

The desktop Outlook shows buttons in the ribbon. (The options to the left are in OWA found under the settings gear to the right in the command bar.)

The apps can also be reached from the welcome message in the group inbox.

9.5.1 Mailbox Apps

Three of the Office 365 Group apps, Conversations Calendar and People, show up in each group member's personal Office 365 mailbox.

You can easily switch between the inbox and the calendar with the links under the group name in the mailbox main area. To see People you must go to that group under your personal contacts.

9.5.1.1 Conversations

In Office 365 Groups the term "Conversations" means e-mail threads. (In Teams and Yammer it refers to chats where several people can join, *see* chapter 12.)

When you create an Office 365 Group, its inbox will be displayed under 'Groups' in each group member's mailbox. E-mails sent to the group e-mail address (that was created at the same time as the group) will end up in this inbox.

Hover the mouse over the text 'Start a conversation' in the e-mail that was sent to welcome you to the group to see the e-mail address, or right click on the text to copy it. (Also the group creator receives such a welcoming e-mail.)

You can forward e-mails to the group inbox, for example if you receive an e-mail in your personal inbox that is interesting to the whole group.

In OWA you can drag and drop the e-mail from the inbox to the group if you don't want to keep a copy for yourself.

The inbox can also receive messages from people outside the group and from outside the organization. This is useful for example when the group is used for problem reporting, or when input about a project plan or similar is needed from non-members or people outside the tenant.

Note that the shared group inbox is not the same as a shared mailbox; *refer to* 5.3.2. It is intended to be an inbox where e-mails can be received and seen by the group. It does not have its own sender address.

9.5.1.2   Calendar

The group calendar is reached through each group member's personal calendar under 'Groups'. Events created in a group calendar, will be displayed there and in each group member's personal calendar.

9.5.1.3   People

When a group member selects the group in his or her personal mailbox contacts in OWA, the people in the group will be displayed and more group members can be added; *refer to* 9.8.1.

9.5.2   SharePoint Site

Each Office 365 Group has a modern SharePoint team site for the group, *refer to* 6.5.1.1, where users can create different kinds of apps and site pages.

9.5.2.1   Files

The group can share and store files in the SharePoint site's default document library, 'Documents'.

The 'Documents' library in the group team site, is displayed in Outlook Web App in a limited version called 'Files'. It shows the same files as the 'Documents' library, but the files lack categorization.

Folders are not displayed, even if the files are grouped in folders in the 'Documents' library. No other columns than the default ones can be added, and those columns cannot be filtered.

'Files' also has less options in the command bar. You can only create a new Word, Excel or PowerPoint file, upload one file at a time and choose whether to display the files as tiles or in a list view.

Because of these limitations, 'Files' has a 'Browse library' link to the 'Documents' library in to the right in the command bar.

Users who visit the library from a desktop Outlook will reach the 'Documents' library in the group team site directly.

9.5.3 Planner

In the group's Planner site, tasks can be created, assigned and managed. Planner has its own chapter in this book, *refer to* 10.

9.5.4 OneNote

An Office 365 Group also has a OneNote app for the group's common notes and information.

Demo:

http://www.kalmstrom.com/Tips/Office-365-Course/Groups.htm

9.6 CONNECTORS

In the group's welcoming message there is a link icon and the text 'Connect your apps'.

When you click on the icon or text, you will be directed to a page where you can connect the group to many different cloud services. Any group member can add a service and let filtered information from that service be added to the shared inbox.

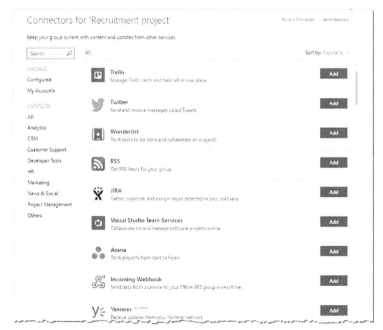

9.7 GROUP MANAGEMENT

The person who creates an Office 365 Group will by default be the group owner. All other group members within the organization will get edit permission over the apps and files used by the group.

By default, all Office 365 users can create groups in their Outlook mailboxes. Most users can organize and manage the groups themselves, but an administrator can also create and delete groups and members in the Office 365 Admin center.

9.7.1 OWA

In OWA, the Group settings are found under the settings gear in the right part of the group command bar.

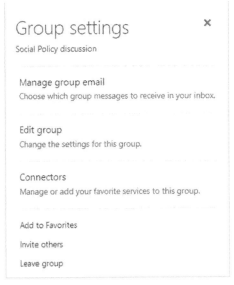

Group members who are *not owners*, will not see the 'Edit group' option.

When you click on 'Edit group', an Edit pane will open to the left of the Group settings pane. Here you can upload a group photo to make the group easier to recognize. You can also change name, description, privacy level and language and set e-mailing options for guests and group messages. For removal of the group, *see* below.

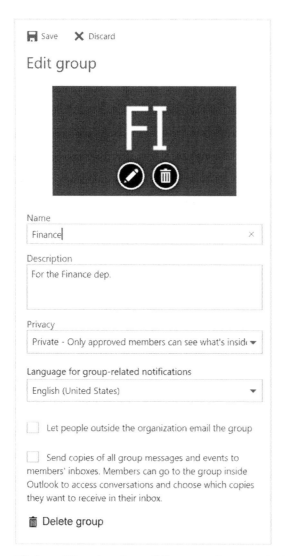

Click on 'Save' on top of the pane to execute the changes.

9.7.2 Outlook

In desktop Outlook, there is an 'Edit Group' button in the ribbon.

The 'Edit Group' button opens a dialog, where group owners can make the same changes as described in OWA above.

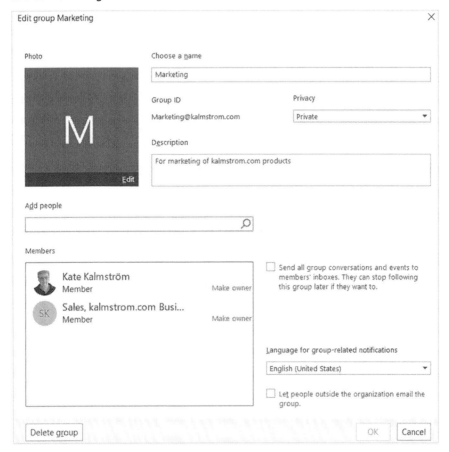

The Outlook dialog also gives a possibility to add new members and to remove current members or make them group owners.

9.7.3 Delete a Group

In the Edit pane/dialog, the owner can delete a group, when it is no longer needed. This will free up system resources, and the group will no longer be listed or displayed.

At the bottom of the Edit pane or dialog, click on the 'Delete group' button. You will be asked to check a box to confirm that you understand that everything will be permanently deleted.

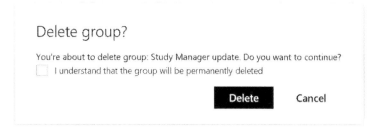

When you delete a group, the group's team site, conversations, e-mails, files, events and any other related information will also be deleted. A deleted group can however be restored via the Exchange Admin center within 30 days; *refer to* 9.9.1.

9.8 MEMBERS MANAGEMENT

The group owner can remove members and change their roles. All members can view information about other members.

9.8.1 OWA Members Page

To reach the OWA Members page, you can use the member count or the settings gear. You can also click on 'People' in the navigation bar under the folders list and select the group.

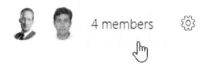

A Members page will open.

Click on the member photo or icon to see information about that member.

The group owner can remove members from the group and also make another member group owner. Hover over the member in the Members page, to see the ellipsis.

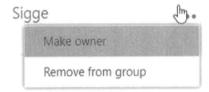

The desktop version of Outlook gives the remove and make owner options in the Edit Group dialog; *refer to* 9.7.2 above.

9.8.2   Add Members

If you choose to create a private group, you need to add members to it manually. This can be done in several ways, but common for all methods is that the group owner must approve members who are added by members who are not owners.

Different kinds of groups that are used within the tenant, including Office 365 Groups, can also be added in the same way.

When an Office 365 Group is used with another Office 365 service, group members can be added directly from that service. I have already described how to add members when you start by creating a modern team site, *refer to* 6.5.1.1, and you will see more examples further on in this book.

9.8.2.1   Add from OWA

There are two ways to add new members from OWA:

• Open the Members page, *see* above, and click on the 'Add members' button.

In the right pane that opens, search for people within your organization by their name or email address. Select the names to add among the suggestions. You can also add e-mail addresses to external users.

- Click on the settings gear to the right in the command bar to open the right pane with group settings.

Click on 'Invite others' to share an invitation link. In the dialog that opens you can either copy the link or click on 'Email' to send the link by e-mail.

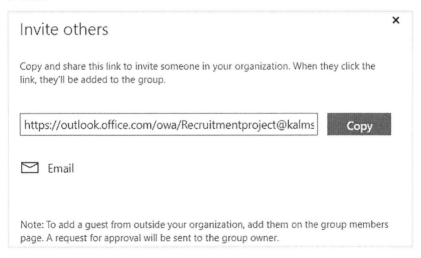

9.8.2.2   Add From Outlook

From a desktop Outlook, click on 'Add Members' in the ribbon group of the selected Office 365 group.

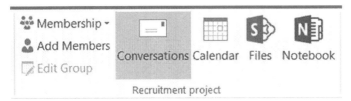

A dialog will open where you can search for and add members in the same ways as in OWA, *see* above.

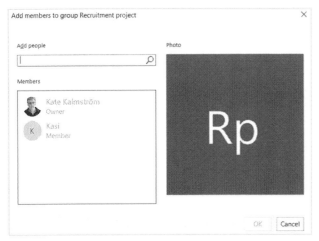

Group owners can also add members from the 'Edit Group' dialog; *refer to* 9.7.2.

9.8.2.3   Guest access

Guests – a person outside the company – cannot access any group, neither private nor public, without an invitation. All invitation methods described above can be used for guests.

Once the invitation has been accepted, the guest can participate in group conversations, receive and respond to calendar invitations and view the group files and the Notebook via links.

9.9   OFFICE 365 ADMIN CENTER GROUPS DASHBOARD

Office 365 administrators can manage groups via the Admin center. Select the group icon and then 'Groups' in the left pane.

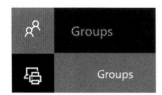

Groups can also be managed from the The Exchange Admin center, *refer to* 5.1. Click on 'groups' under the 'recipients' heading.

recipients

mailboxes

groups

resources

Administrators can delete and restore groups, add and remove owners as well as regular group members and edit the group settings.

The admin can also create a new group and select an owner for it. The administrator does not have to be included in the group to perform these operations.

Under Settings >Services & add-ins >Office 365 Groups administrators can restrict the possibility to invite people from outside the company to groups.

9.9.1 Restore a Deleted Group

A deleted Office 365 group is retained for 30 days. During this "soft-delete" period, admins can still restore the group from the Exchange Admin center. After 30 days, the group and associated content cannot be restored.

These are the steps to restore a soft-deleted group:

1. In the Exchange Admin center, click on 'groups' under the 'recipients' heading.

2. Select the group you want to restore. A right information pane will open.

Marketing

Office 365 group
Marketing@kalmstrom.com

Status

This group was deleted on 2/17/2018 4:47:56 PM

Click here to restore ⬅━━━

3. Click on the restore link.

4. Confirm.

Demo:

https://www.kalmstrom.com/Tips/Office-365-Course/Groups.htm

9.10 SUMMARY

Office 365 Groups is an important feature and some useful services build on Groups, so I hope my introduction has made you understand how groups work and which apps are shared within a group.

You should also know how each user can create and manage a group and how groups can be managed through the Office 365 Admin center.

Now we will take a look at some apps that use Office 365 Groups.

10 PLANNER

Planner is a planning tool connected to Office 365 Groups. The
Planner icon is visible to all users in the Office 365 App
Launcher without any actions from the administrator. You
can also access Planner on iOS and Android devices.

When you click on the Planner tile, you are directed to the Planner hub
at https://tasks.office.com/. Here users can share plans and tasks, and
each user can reach his/her own tasks from 'My tasks' in the left pane.

Planner has virtually no customization possibilities at all. There are a few
controls in a left pane and a few more on each plan's board, but that is
all. For more advanced tasks and project management, I recommend a
SharePoint based solution instead.

On the other hand, Planner is very straightforward and easy to use. Each
plan has its own board, where users can create tasks and categorize
them in "buckets".

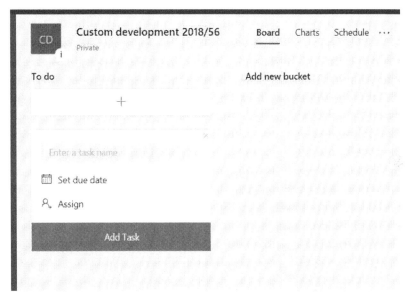

10.1 PLANNER AND GROUPS

When a plan is created, Office 365 also creates a new Office 365 Group
with the same name as the plan, so that colleagues who work on the
same plan can collaborate and share information.

The group's files, notebook and site can be reached from the ellipsis to
the right of the Schedule link in the open plan. Planner has no direct link
to the group calendar, but instead a link to the OWA Members page;
refer to 9.8.1.

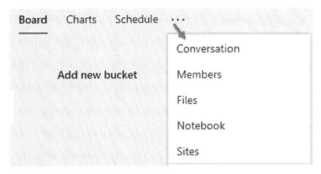

It is the other way around too, as described above in chapter 9: When you create an Office 365 Group from Outlook, a plan with the same name as the group is automatically created and shared among the members of this group.

Users can see all plans they are members of when they click on 'Planner Hub' in Planner's left pane, no matter how each plan was created.

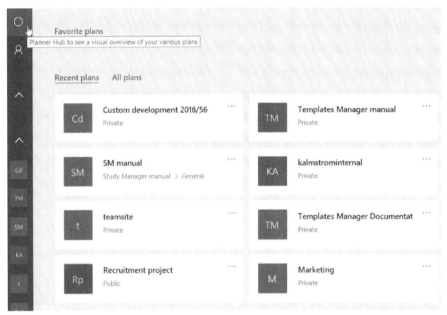

10.2 PLANS

A Planner "plan" is actually a goal that you want to achieve or a project you are working on, and in Planner users can see and manage the various tasks and steps you and your colleagues have to perform to reach the goal or finish the project.

10.2.1 Create a Plan

The first time you access Planner, a dialog where you are asked to create a plan comes up. Give the plan a name (and a description) and decide if it should be public – open to all the tenant's users – which is default, or if it should be open only to people you invite.

Check the subscription box at the bottom of the dialog if you want to automatically make every new member 'Follow the plan'; *refer to* 10.2.2.1 below.

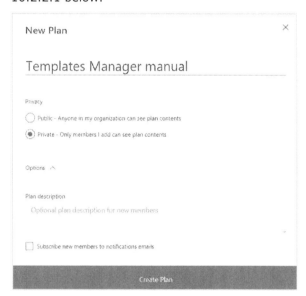

After that first time, you can create new plans via the '+ New Plan' command in Planner's left pane.

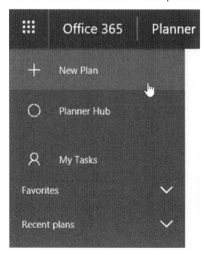

10.2.2 Plan Notifications

Planner can send notifications to the group inbox as well as too each members personal inbox.

10.2.2.1   Alerts To All

When you click on the ellipsis to the right of the Schedule tab in the open board, you will find multiple links and among them 'Edit Plan'. (The person who created the plan cannot leave it, so 'Leave Plan' is only visible to other plan members.)

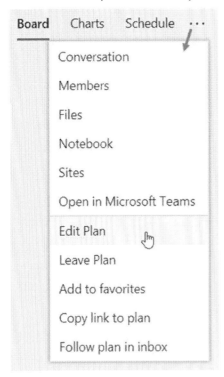

When you click on 'Edit Plan', a dialog will open. Here you can turn on notifications to the inbox of the plan's Office 365 Group when any task has been assigned and completed. This feature is off by default.

When you click on 'Follow plan in inbox', you will receive these notifications for all directly in your personal inbox as well, except in cases when you yourself assign a task to someone else.

The link text will be changed into 'Stop following plan in inbox', so that you can click on it again if you find that there are too many e-mails. (This only applies if the auto-subscription box was left unchecked at plan creation, see 11.2.1 above.)

10.2.2.2 Alerts to Single Members

Each Plan member can click on the settings gear in the Office 365 right navigation bar above an open plan and set personal notification options.

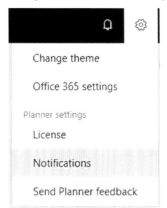

The notifications are enabled by default, so if you don't uncheck the boxes you will have e-mails when you are assigned a task and when a task assigned to you is late, due today or due in the next 7 days.

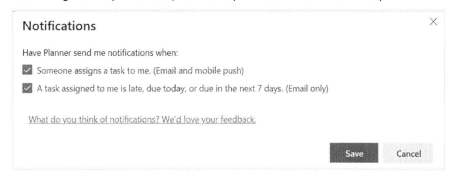

10.3 BOARD

When you click on one of the plans in the Planner Hub, the plan opens in Board view, *see also* the first image in this chapter. This is where you most often work with and categorize the tasks.

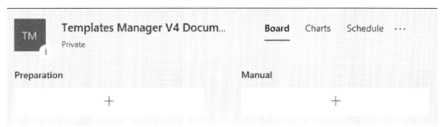

To the right in the command bar, you can see plan members and filter the tasks by keyword, due date, color label or assignment. You can also group the buckets by several parameters.

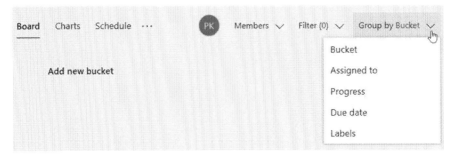

10.3.1 Task Categorization

Users can categorize and group the different tasks of the plan by placing them in buckets. Tasks can also be marked with colored labels.

10.3.1.1 Buckets

For most plans it is best to use multiple buckets, to find tasks more easily. Tasks can be dragged and dropped within and between buckets.

To create a new bucket, click on 'Add new bucket' to the right of the existing buckets.

Type or paste a name and press Enter on the keyboard to add the new bucket to the plan.

To rename a bucket, click in the name and write the new name. You may also hover the mouse over the bucket name to show the ellipsis and click on 'Rename'.

Under the ellipsis you can also delete the bucket and re-arrange the order of the buckets. Buckets to the left will have the command 'Move right' instead of 'Move left' as in the image below.

10.3.1.2   Colored Labels

Tasks cannot only be categorized in buckets. Each task can also have a colored label attached to it. There are six colors, and you can write any label names you wish for them, but you cannot change the colors or add more labels.

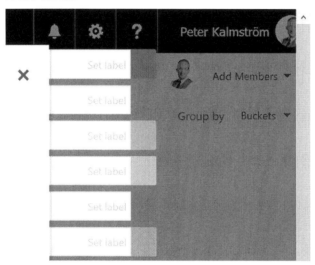

To set labels, open a task and type the labels you wish to use. The same labels will then be visible in all tasks in that plan.

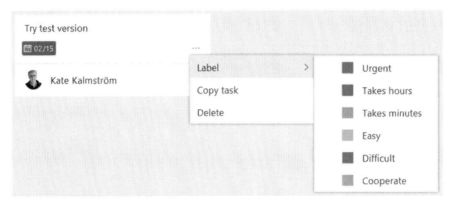

You can combine color labels and use more than one. For example, you could have colors for priority and combine them with colors for how long time a task is estimated to take. Then each task would have two tabs, one for priority and one for duration.

10.3.2 Manage Tasks

When a new plan has no tasks, there is by default a 'To Do' bucket, with an empty new task.

10.3.2.1 Create a New Task

To create the first task, enter a task name in the open task in the 'To Do' bucket and click on 'Add task' – or press Enter – to add the new task to the 'To Do' bucket. (You can of course change the bucket name, see 10.3.1.1. above.) The task will now be displayed as a task card that contains the most important task information.

You can also set a due date for the task and/or assign a responsible person, but that may as well be done later.

Click on the plus sign under the bucket name to create subsequent tasks in the same bucket.

10.3.2.2 Edit a Task

Click on the task card in the bucket to open it. Now you can set dates and assign a responsible. You can also create subtasks, add a description, attachments and links and add a comment that also will be sent to the group inbox.

There is no saving in this dialog. Changes will be saved automatically. Click outside the pane or use the x in the upper right corner to close the task form. However, comments have to be posted with the 'Send' button.

When you write a description and add subtasks, checkboxes for 'Show on card' will be visible. Check one of them if you want the description or the open subtasks to be visible on the task card. (You cannot check both.)

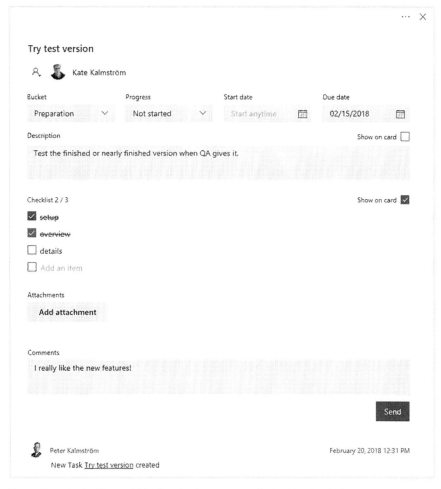

From top to bottom, this is what you can do in the task form.

- Assign the task to yourself or to another group member. When you assign the task to another person, he/she will have a message about it in their personal Office 365 mailbox.

- Under the ellipsis: copy or delete the task.

- Select Progress status – Not started, In progress and Completed.

- Set Start and Due date for the task.

- Add subtasks to the task under 'Checklist'.

  o To add a new subtask, click on 'add an item' and start writing. Click outside the field when you are finished.

  o When the subtask has been completed, check the box to the left of the subtask name, and the name will be crossed-out automatically. Uncheck the box again if you want to reopen the subtask.

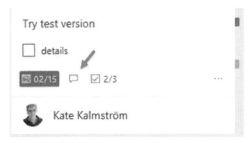

  o In the card image above, the 'Show on card' box has been checked for the checklist, and two subtasks of three has been completed. The task is assigned to Kate Kalmström and is categorized by two colored tabs. It has at least one comment (the icon at the arrow). The completed checkboxes and the subtask names are only shown when 'Show on card' has been checked.

- Add a description of the task.

- Add attachments from SharePoint or PC or add a link.

- Add a comment. A comment icon will be added to the task card, and the comment will also be sent to the group inbox.

10.3.2.3   Mark a Task as Completed

Hover over the task card to display the completed icon. Click on the icon to mark the task as completed.

150

Completed tasks can still be seen in the bucket. Click on 'Show completed' under the active tasks to show the cards for the completed tasks.

When you hover over the completed task card, a restore icon is displayed. Click on it to open the task again.

10.3.2.4 Delete a Task

In the open task, click on the ellipsis in the top right corner to delete the task.

10.4 CHARTS

Under the 'Charts' tab, you can see a graphic representation of the plan's tasks.

The 'Charts' area shows all task statuses to the left and statuses for each plan member to the right.

In a pane further to the right, there is a list of all tasks. The tasks in this right pane can be grouped in various ways.

You can create new tasks directly from the charts page by clicking on the plus sign on top of the list of tasks to the right.

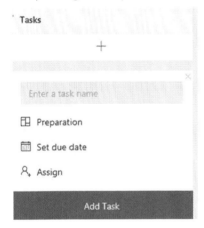

Click on the entries to set bucket and due date and to assign the task.

10.5 SCHEDULE

Under the 'Schedule' tab, the tasks in the open plan are displayed in a calendar, which can be shown in Week or Month view.

In the calendar you will get an overview of all the tasks and their distribution over time. Click on a task to open it directly from the calendar.

10.5.1 Stretch Due Date

It is easy to set a task's due date to a later date by dragging. (If you try to set it to an earlier date, the task will open so that you can make the change in the task form.)

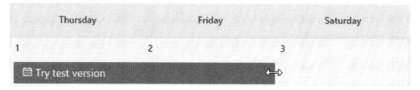

10.5.2 Unscheduled Tasks

To the right of the calendar, there is a pane with unscheduled tasks, grouped by bucket. Drag tasks to the applicable time slot to schedule them.

Tasks in the calendar can also be dragged to a bucket in the 'Unscheduled tasks' pane. They will then lose their date entries.

153

10.5.3 Create Tasks

When you hover with the mouse cursor over a date, a plus sign will be visible. Click on it to create a new task in the same way as under the Chart tab, *see* above. There is no due date selection here. Instead you can drag the task to the suitable due date after creation.

You can also create new tasks from the 'Unscheduled tasks' pane, *see* above. If you set a due date on that task, it will immediately be displayed in the calendar. Otherwise it will stay under 'Unscheduled tasks'

Demo:

https://kalmstrom.com/Tips/Office-365-Course/Planner.htm

10.6   SUMMARY

Planner is a user friendly way to handle simple tasks management. In this chapter we have looked at notification options and task categorization possibilities, and you have learned how to manage buckets, tasks and subtasks.

We have also studied the chart view and the calendar, and I have explained the connection between Planner and Office 365 Groups.

Microsoft will soon roll out a new feature which allows users to see their Planner tasks in Outlook using the iCalendar format.

11 STREAM

Microsoft Stream is a new video service that will replace the earlier Office 365 Video. Therefore this chapter replaces the Video chapter in earlier versions of this book.

The fully featured Stream – Plan 2 – is only available in the E5 subscriptions, but a Plan 2 add-on can be added to other licenses for an extra fee. I recommend that you first take advantage of the free trial; *refer to* https://stream.microsoft.com/pricing.

In this chapter, I have used the Stream edition that is included in the E3 subscription. By default, Stream is available for all users in the Enterprise subscriptions.

Stream stores videos and metadata in its own service, built on top of Microsoft Azure. 500 GB storage + 0.5 GB per licensed user is allowed, and more storage can be added. Only the original file sizes are counted.

When you click on the Stream icon in the App Launcher, you will be directed to https://web.microsoftstream.com, where you can upload, watch and manage videos. Stream works well with other Office 365 apps like PowerApps, Flow and SharePoint.

11.1 UPLOAD VIDEOS

Videos can be uploaded to Stream in the same way as you upload files to a SharePoint library or a video to YouTube: click on the upload icon and select or drag and drop the video file.

Drag files here, or select files to upload

The first time you upload a video you will be asked to select the video language. This language setting will be default for future uploads but can be changed in the video settings, *see* below.

You will have an e-mail to your Office 365 mailbox when the upload has been finished.

While the video is uploading you can make various settings for it. The dialog comes up automatically when the upload has begun, and it has three parts. At the bottom, there are buttons for sharing and publication.

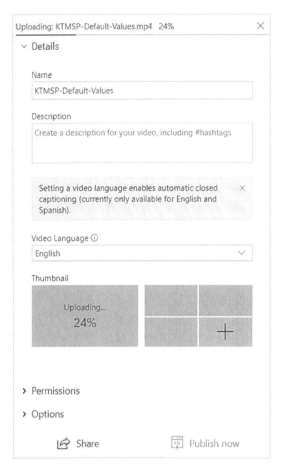

If you want to edit the settings later, select 'My videos' under 'My content' in the command bar.

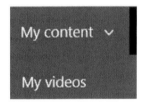

Now you will see all your videos and information about them. Click on the pen icon far to the right to edit the video settings.

11.1.1 Details

Stream has some advanced features that are set under 'Details':

- When you enter hashtags in the Description, viewers can click on them to reach other videos with the same tags. Format: #kanban

- If you add time codes in the Description, viewers can click on them to jump to the part of the video they are most interested in. Format: 0:50

- There is an automatic speech-to-text transcript, currently English and Spanish.

Under 'Details' you can also select one of the automatically created thumbnails or upload your own.

11.1.2 Permissions

By default, everyone in the organization is allowed to watch, edit and even remove your video. Uncheck the box and limit the permission by using the 'Shared with' dropdown. Here you can search for groups, channels or persons who should share the video.

When you limit the permissions, you can give more people than yourself the possibility to edit the video, by making them video owners.

The Display box is used to display videos to Stream groups or channels, and it is checked by default when you select to share with a group or channel.

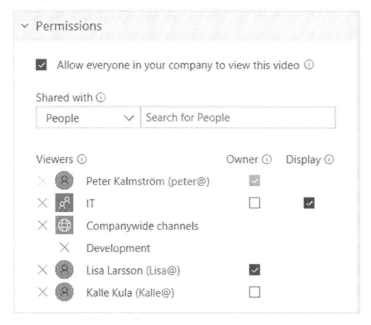

11.1.3 Options

Under Options you can decide if comments should be allowed and if a caption file should be generated automatically (currently only for English and Spanish).

You can also upload your own subtitles file.

11.2 ORGANIZE VIDEOS

The videos can be placed in different channels, and you can also create Microsoft Stream Office 365 Groups, *see* below.

Another way to group videos is to add them to your watchlist. All this can be reached from the command bar, My content. Here you can also reach the videos you have uploaded and the channels you are following.

Channels and groups can be created either from the 'My channels' and 'My groups' pages or via links under 'Create' in the command bar.

11.2.1 Add Video to Group or Channel

To add a video to a Group or Channel, open 'My videos' and click on the add icon.

Here you can select and search for group, channel and also add people.

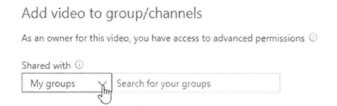

11.2.2 Groups

Use Stream groups when you want to limit access to your videos. By default the group is private and members are allowed to edit the videos. If you disable contribution, the group members cannot be made video owners; *refer to* 11.1.2.

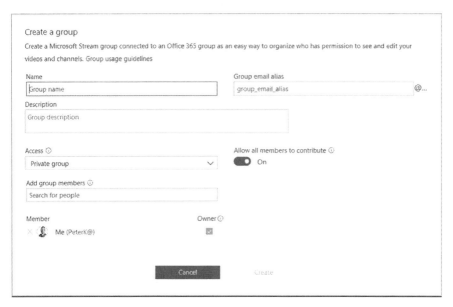

A Stream group, it is acually an Office 365 Group, *refer to* chapter 9, so you can use the Stream group in various ways across Office 365. Existing Office 365 Groups where you are a member will also show up among your groups in Stream.

Each Office 365 Group, either it is created in Stream or elsewhere, gets its own mini-portal.

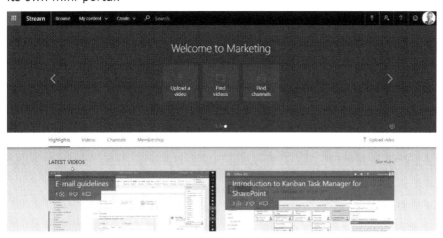

From here you can watch and create videos and channels, see highlighted content and change memberships and roles.

11.2.3 Channels

Stream channels are good for arranging videos by topic. Users can follow channels by clicking on a 'Follow' button, *see* the image in the next section below.

When you create a new channel, you can decide if it should be a companywide channel (default) or if access to the channel should be limited to a group or to just a few people.

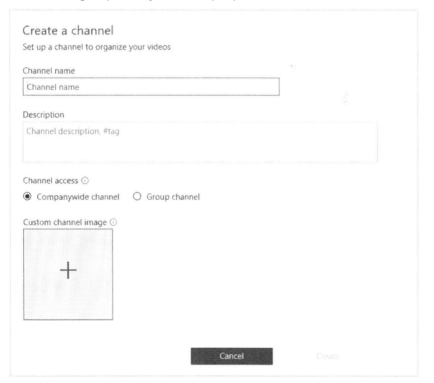

11.3 SEARCH

You can search for content in Stream from Search box at the top of any page. All content in Office 365 is security trimmed, so if you don't have access to a video, channel or group it won't show up in Stream or your search results.

You can search among Videos, Channels, People and Groups, and the hits can be sorted in various ways. If you cannot see the search options, write something in the search field in the command bar and press Enter.

When you search for 'People' you can click on the hits and see and edit that person's videos and channels – if they are companywide or you have been given access to them in other ways, of course.

The Video search goes through the autogenerated video transcripts in all videos. If there is a hit, you can click on it to get to the part of the video where the word was found.

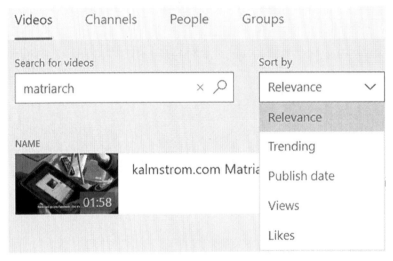

The video search can also be performed on only one video. In that case, the search box can be found above the transcript, to the right of the open video.

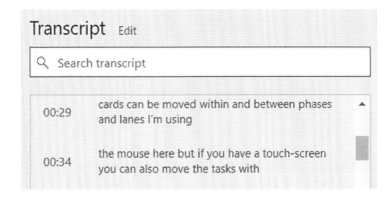

11.3.1 Edit transcripts

To have best possible search results, you should edit the transcripts. Click on 'Edit' above the search box, *see* the image above, and select the text you want to edit.

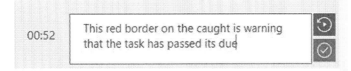

In the transcript above, the word "caught" should be replaced with "card", and "a" should be inserted before "warning".

11.4 SHARE VIDEOS

You can share videos by copying the URL from the video page and pasting it in an e-mail or chat message, but if you use the Share button you will have more options. The Share button looks the same in all Office 365.

In Stream you can find the Share button above each video. Share buttons can also be found under the ellipsis on each video under 'My videos' and 'My watchlist'.

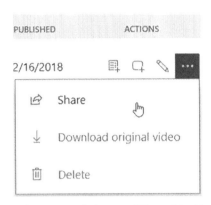

When you click on a 'Share' button, a dialog with three tabs will open:

- Share with a link. Under this tab also get the option to start the sharing a bit into the video and to share the link on Yammer.

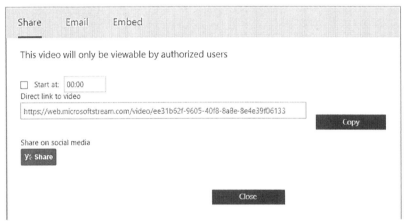

- E-mail a link to the video. Here you can add people who should receive a link to the video, and the e-mail will be sent automatically.

- Embed the video. Here too, you will have a 'Start at' option, and there are also some size settings and settings for autoplay, responsiveness and info.

Permissions will be kept when you share videos from Stream, and unauthorized people who try to view a shared video that they don't have access to will have an error message.

11.4.1 Share Channels

There are Share buttons and on each channel under 'My channels' and 'Followed channels', and you can also use the URL to the channel page. The Share buttons give a link and an embed option.

11.4.2 The SharePoint Stream Web Part

Modern SharePoint pages have a web part where you can easily insert a video from the Microsoft Stream. Click on the plus sign on the page in edit mode and select the Stream web part.

A right pane will open, where you can enter the URL to a video or channel and select if the link points to a single video or a channel. Then you can publish the page and watch the video in SharePoint.

11.4.3 Stream Videos in Other Apps

The web part in modern SharePoint pages is not the only way to integrate Stream in another Office 365 app. Here are some suggestions:

- Embed a video in a SharePoint Online wiki page.

- In Teams channels, add tabs with Stream videos or channels.

- In Yammer, paste a Stream video link into a conversation, or use the button in the Share dialog, see 11.4 above.

- In OneNote, paste a Stream video link into a page or select Insert->Online Video and paste the URL.

- In Sway click on the plus sign to create a new card and select Media >Embed. Paste the Sway video embed code in the card. (There is a video option, but currently it is not connected to Stream.)

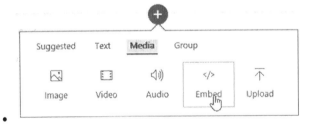

-

11.5 SETTINGS

The Stream settings can be reached from the profile picture in the top right corner.

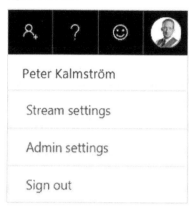

11.5.1 *Users' Stream Settings*

All users have the Stream settings. Here you can turn off and on e-mail notifications that are sent by the system when video upload processing is completed and when a video has been shared with you. This feature is activated by default.

You can also set language and region and have a link to the organization's policy for Stream usage, if it has been uploaded in the Admin settings.

11.5.2 *Admin Stream Settings*

From start only Global Tenant Administrators have an 'Admin settings' link under the profile picture. Global Admins can assign Stream administrator rights to others, and then they will also get the 'Admin settings' link.

In the page that opens, many settings can be administered. The image below shows the left pane, where options are selected.

	Administrators: Make people or groups Stream admins – or remove them.
⚙ Admin settings	
👤 Administrators	Content creation: By default all users can create videos and channels, but here you can restrict that to only specified people or groups.
╋ Content creation	
✳ Spotlight videos	Spotlight videos: Add 1-4 videos to be displayed under the command bar on the Stream home page.
🗩 Comments	Comments: By default, users are allowed to comment on videos. This feature can be disabled here.
👥 Groups	Groups: Links to the Office 365 Admin center and the Azure portal, where you can manage Office 365 groups.
🛡 Company policies	Company policies: Give a link to the policies for Stream usage. You can also make it mandatory to accept the policies before a video can be uploaded.
◔ Usage details	Usage details: Keep track of storage space.
? Support	Support: Submit a support ticket.

Demo:

https://www.kalmstrom.com/Tips/Office-365-Course/Stream.htm

11.6 SUMMARY

The Stream portal is a place for videos from the whole tenant, available to all users or to selected groups. In this chapter we have seen how Stream is connected to Office 365 Groups and looked at the video categorization and settings.

After studying this chapter I hope you understand the Stream customization and search options and know how to share videos to other apps, so that you can take advantage of the possibilities for your organization.

12 TEAMS AND YAMMER – CONVERSATION APPS

Office 365 has two apps for chats and conversations, one very new and one older that is presently under re-construction: Teams and Yammer. You can chat and share files and notes in both of them, but there are important differences. The most optimal, at least for a bigger organization, might be to use both but in different contexts.

Microsoft Teams is suitable for small groups that have a relatively short life span, for example groups that are created for cooperation on a specific project. Yammer groups are typically managed by someone that customizes the organization's Yammer site and fosters participation over time.

Small groups can collaborate in a single Team, but too many users will make it noisy and of little use. A team can not have more than 999 members, and for smooth function I advise that you have considerably less than so.

Yammer groups, on the other hand, are more like a forum. They can reach the entire enterprise, and their value increases with the number of nodes.

If you need to get a quick group of collaborators together around a specific goal, Microsoft Teams is the right tool, but if you're trying to build a community, Yammer is a better choice.

Once a project team has come together to work on a specific set of task, they should decide whether to use Teams or Yammer to get their specific work done. I don't recommend using both for the same project.

Which option you prefer depends on several elements. Among those are:

- The content of the conversations. Should the conversations be available for the group lifetime, or should they live on after it, or even become a much wider group? In the latter case, Yammer is to be preferred.

- Project size and duration. Is the project small and expected to last a short time only? In that case you might prefer the user friendliness of Teams.

- Video conferences. If video conferences will be an important part of the work, Teams is convenient and to prefer over Yammer.

I will give an overview over both apps, and I hope it will help you make useful choices.

12.1 TEAMS

Everyone who is used to Skype chats or other chat applications will quickly understand how Teams works. Here I will describe the browser version of Teams, but there is also a Teams desktop app and apps for iOS, Android and Windows Phone.

The Office apps as well as various other applications can be reached from within Teams. Skype for Business is also integrated for voice and video conferences, but the chat part is totally Office 365.

When a new team is created, a new Office 365 Group is created automatically, including the group SharePoint site, mailbox, calendar and Planner. If a team is activated on an existing group, *refer to* 12.1.3.1, the existing services for that group are used instead.

12.1.1 Admin Management

Teams settings can be managed on tenant level in the Office 365 Admin center. It is also here that you enable and disable Teams for the organization and for guests. By default, Teams is enabled for the organization and disabled for guests.

1. In the Offce 365 Admin center, expand the Settings and click on 'Services & add-ins'.

2. Click on 'Microsoft Teams'.

3. A right pane will open, where you can enable and disable Teams by clicking on the On/Off button. There is one setting for the tenant and one for guests. The tenant setting is on by default, while the guest setting is off.

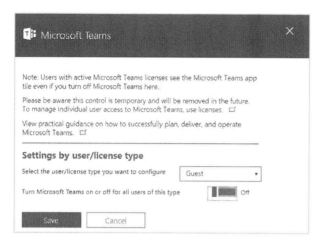

4. When Teams is on, you will have many more settings options. You can for example turn off external apps (under Apps) or private chats (under Messaging), which is on by default, or allow team owners to delete all messages, which is off by default.

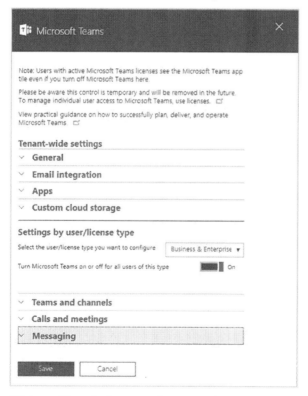

5. Click on 'Save' when you have made your settings.

12.1.2 The Teams Site

When users click on the Teams tile in the Office 365 home page or in the App Launcher, they will be directed to their Teams home page at https://teams.microsoft.com.

The Teams pages have three parts. There is a left pane with commands and a middle pane, which gives choices connected to the left pane selection.

The main area is to the right, and it is here the activity takes place. Its content depends on what you have selected to the left. From start, the main area has prompts to action, but later it will be filled with conversations or information.

12.1.2.1   Left Pane

The Teams left pane has links to information about all teams you are a member of. The information will be shown in the middle pane, to the right of the left pane. You can also select to see notifications about your recent activity, private chats, meetings, files and apps.

Here is what the buttons show in the middle pane:

Activity: mentions, likes and replies.

Chat: a list of all your private conversations.

Teams: a list of teams where you are a member.

Meetings: upcoming meetings, an agenda and meeting scheduling.

Files: each user's recent files, Team's files and files on OneDrive for Business. More cloud storages can be added.

Store: Microsoft Store.

Feedback: suggest enhancements, comment on suggestions and vote.

12.1.2.1.1 *Ellipsis Options*

Under the left pane ellipsis, users can have apps easy at hand for use in Teams. You can for example select Planner to quickly see "My Tasks", or OneNote for both personal and team notes.

The 'Who' app lets you find information about other people in the organization. You can for example search for people with certain skills or just search for info about a certain person. The first time you use 'Who', you have to install it. When you have installed 'Who', it will also be visible among your private chats.

Apps you don't need can be uninstalled. Just select the app and then click on 'Uninstall' under the app ellipsis. You can also add more apps.

12.1.3 Create a New Team

A team is a collection of people, content and tools for different projects and purposes within an organization. By default, all users can create a team, but the creation settings defined by Office 365 Groups apply to Teams also.

The user who creates a team becomes the team owner, and only this person can add and remove other team members.

To create a new team, select the 'Teams' icon in the left pane and click on the 'Create and join team' link at the bottom of the middle pane.

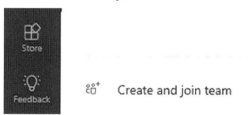

Now the main area will give a choice of public teams you can join, and there is also a 'Create a team' button.

173

Give the team a name and a description and select if it should be a private or public team. Click on 'Next'.

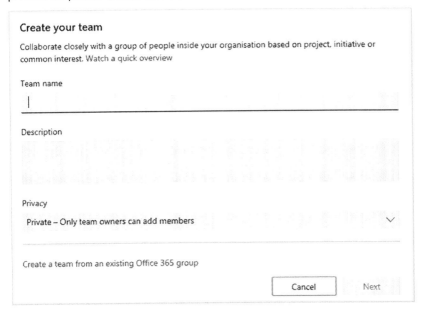

An Office 365 Group with the team name will now be added to the global address book. It can be selected as other people and groups, so people added to the team can be added as a group to other Office 365 apps as well.

When the team has been created you can see its name to the middle pane when you click on the Teams icon in the left pane.

A "General" channel for chats with all team members will also be created, *refer to* 12.1.5.3.

12.1.3.1   Create from Office 365 Group

If you are the administrator of a private Office 365 Group (of less than 2500 people), you can add Teams among the other apps in an already existing group, instead of creating the team and group as described above.

The people in the existing group will be added to the new team automatically, and the existing Outlook and SharePoint functionality will be added to the team.

Click on the link 'Create a team from an existing Office 365 group' at the bottom of the Create team dialog, *see* the image above. Then select the group where you want to add Teams.

Note that you can only link to an existing Office 365 Group when you create a new team – it cannot be done after the team has been created.

12.1.3.2   Add Team Members

When the team has been created, you are asked to add team members. Start writing the name of a person or group and select the correct one among the suggestions. Then click on Add. (For people outside the organization; *refer to* 12.1.4.1.1.)

You can also skip this step in the team creation and add team members later, *see* 12.1.4 below.

Click on 'Done' when you have added enough team members for now.

Each person who has been added to a team will receive an e-mail about it, with a link to the Teams site.

Peter added you to the Folder HelpDesk Kanban Board team!

FH

Folder HelpDesk Kanban Board

3 members

Comment here on the design of the new kanban board in Folder HelpDesk!

Open Microsoft Teams

The message also contains general information about Teams and a link to download Teams apps for desktop and mobile.

Get it now! Take it with you wherever you go.

Windows

iOS

Mac

Android

Windows Phone

Go to downloads page

12.1.4 Owner Management

The person who created the team is its owner, and as an owner this user has more permissions over the team than regular users.

The owner can:

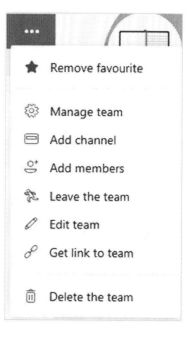

- Add and remove team members and make other team members owners.
- Edit and delete a team.
- Manage various settings for the team.

When a team owner clicks on the ellipsis at the team name, more options will be displayed than for regular users.

(Regular users will only see 'Favorite/Remove favorite', 'Manage team', 'Add channel', 'Leave the team' and 'Get link to team'. The regular users' also get less options under 'Manage team'.)

When a team is deleted, all content is deleted too, just as the Office 365 Group associated with the team, but it can be restored within 30 days. *Refer to* 9.9.1.

When the team owner selects 'Manage team' in the dropdown, a page with four tabs will open in the main area. The 'Members' tab is open by default.

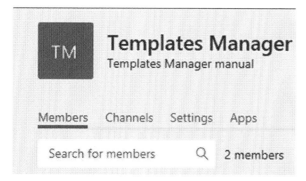

The 'Channels' and 'Apps' tabs lets you manage the channels and apps that are used in the team.

12.1.4.1   Manage Members

Select the 'Manage team' option under the ellipsis at the team name, and all members will be displayed under the 'Members' tab in the main area. Hover over the member you want to change status for or remove from the team.

Change status by selecting the suitable option in the dropdown at the member.

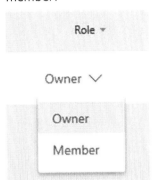

Remove the member from the team by clicking on the x. This user will now be removed from the Office 365 Group associated with the team.

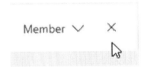

Owners can also add new members from under the Members tab, by the button in the top right corner above the list of existing members.

12.1.4.1.1   *Add Guests*

If guest access to Teams has been enabled for the tenant, *refer to* 12.1.1, you can add people from outside the organization to a team by entering their e-mail address. Guests that do not yet have a Microsoft account associated to their email will be directed to create a Microsoft account for free, as this is required to access the Teams service.

When you have added the e-mail address, be sure to click on the edit icon and enter the proper name of the person. If you don't do that, the part before @ in the e-mail address will be shown to the other team members.

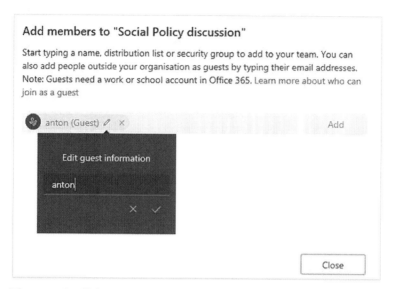

The guest will have an e-mail invitation, and when the guest has joined the team, other users can see the guest presence from the text "This team has guests" under the team name in the main area. A "GUEST" label also appears next to each guest name.

12.1.4.2   Manage Team Settings

Select the 'Manage team' option under the ellipsis at the team name and open the Settings tab. Here the team owner can add a team picture and make many changes in the default team settings.

Members Channels Settings Apps	
▸ **Team picture**	Add a team picture
▸ **Member permissions**	Enable channel creation, adding apps and more
▸ **Guest permissions**	Enable channel creation
▸ **@mentions**	Choose who can use @team and @channel mentions
▸ **Fun stuff**	Allow emoji, memes, GIFs or stickers

12.1.5 Chats

Teams has two chat types: the channels, which can be seen by all team members, and the private chats between selected people.

12.1.5.1 Compose Box

Both chat types use the same kind of compose box.

The Teams chat has more formatting features than most other chats on the market, and you can send files and start or join video meetings directly from within the chat.

The compose box is collapsed by default, and no formatting icons are visible.

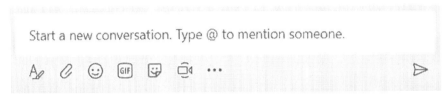

The icon to the right under the box is for posting the chat entry. You can also press Enter on the keyboard.

The icons to the left under the box are, from left to right:

- Edit. When you click on the 'A' icon to the left, the compose box will expand and you can see the formatting options on top.

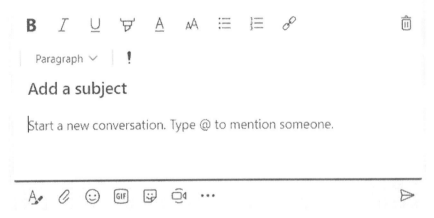

- Attach a file.
- Three icons for emojis, animated gifs and stickers.
- Start a video conference using your PCs webcamera and microphone.
- Under the ellipsis, you can find links to sites outside Teams.

You can for example add a news or Wikipedia article or a YouTube video to the chat.

When you hover over a chat message you have sent, you can see an ellipsis, a Save icon and a Like icon. The ellipsis is only there for 24 hours, and it has three options, Edit, Delete and Mark as unread. After 24 hours it will not longer be possible to edit or delete the message.

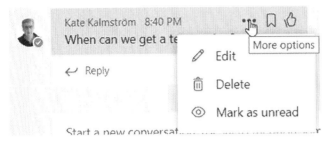

The save icon saves the individual message, so that you can easily find important parts of chat threads. Click on Activity in the left pane and select 'My Activity' in the top left corner of the middle pane to see it. Here you can also study other activity.

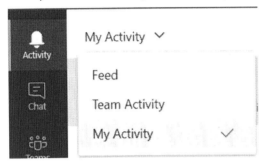

12.1.5.2   Files

You can upload files to Teams in both chat types. Click on the paper clip icon in the compose box and select from where you want to fetch the file.

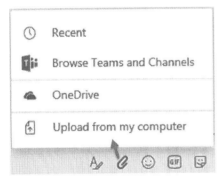

The files can be opened, edited and downloaded in the conversation. You can also have a link to it and create a new channel tab for the file.

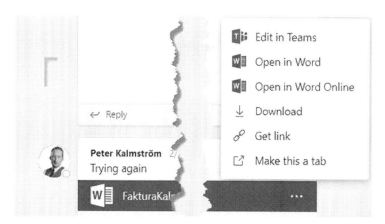

You can also reach the file under the channel's 'Files' tab, *see* below.

Files that have been added to chats can be edited by everyone who can see it, so if you want to give Read-only permission, share the file via OneDrive for Business or SharePoint Online instead.

When you click on a file inside a chat, it opens in preview instead of opening in the chat. In the top right corner you will have the options to Edit (for Office files) or download the file. 'Open in SharePoint' opens the team's SharePoint document library, which was created with the Office 365 Group.

If you click on the 'Show conversation' icon, the chat where the file was added will be displayed to the right. That way you can continue chatting while studying the file.

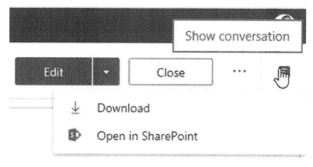

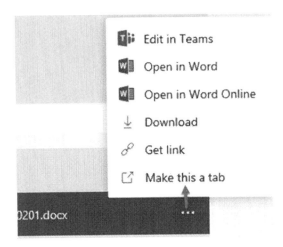

12.1.5.3 Channels

All members of a team share conversations, files, notes and more in the team channels. The team members can see the whole conversation in the main area and join it at any time.

Select 'Teams' in the left pane and then a team and a channel in the middle pane. Now the main area will show the conversation in the selected channel.

The channels is a way of categorizing conversations and keeping them organized. When a team is created there is a 'General' channel created automatically. This channel is default and cannot be deleted.

On top of the main area there are links to the team's files, notes and frequently accessed tools. Use the plus sign to pin content from Office 365 and third party apps here.

12.1.5.3.1 *Conversations Tab*

Select a channel to see the details for that channel in the main area. The 'Conversations' tab, opens by default.

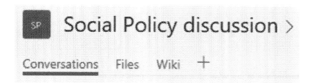

Most of the channel's activity takes place under the 'Conversations' tab, because it is here you see the channel chat.

12.1.5.3.2 Files Tab

The 'Files' tab opens a limited version of the SharePoint library where all files that have been uploaded to the channel are stored. Under the 'Files' tab, you can read and edit the files and create folders and new Office documents.

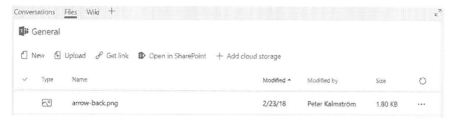

Go to the team's full SharePoint library by selecting 'Open in SharePoint' above the files, under the item ellipsis.

You can also find the command under the channel ellipsis.

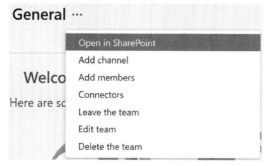

The image above is from a team owner. Other team members do not have as many options, but everyone can open the SharePoint library.

At each file or folder, there is also an ellipsis with options for the selected item.

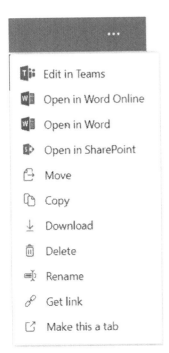

The team's SharePoint library holds files from all the team channels. Each channel has its own folder in the library.

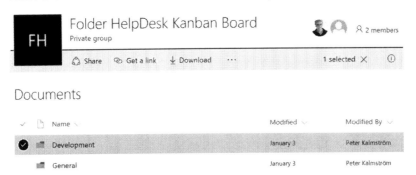

12.1.5.3.3 *Wiki Tab*

The 'Wiki' tab opens a box where members can add notes for the channel. It can for example be important links or other information that you need to have easy at hand in the channel.

The notes can be categorized in pages and sections, so that each page can contain several sections. (Note that OneNote, which is a similar app, has it the other way around: each section can have several pages. *Refer to* 4.1.1.5.)

Add new sections to a page by clicking on the plus icon that is displayed when you hover the mouse under the last existing section.

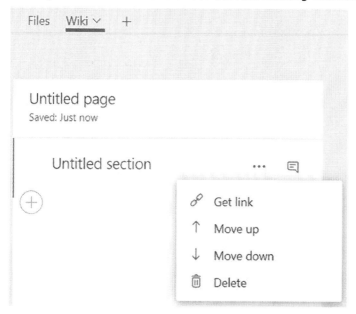

When you hover the mouse over a section name, an ellipsis and a chat icon will be visible to the right. Click on the chat icon to open a chat window. Everything you write there will show up in the channel chat.

There is a table of contents for the wiki pages and sections in the top left corner of the main screen.

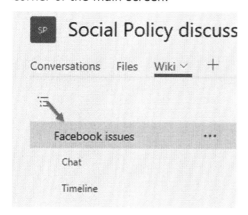

The Wiki notes are stored in a document library called 'Teams Wiki Data' in the SharePoint site that belongs to the team's Office 365 Group.

12.1.5.3.4 *Additional Tabs*

The plus icon to the right of the Wiki tab lets you add a tab for content that you want to have at hand in the channel. It opens a dialog with a lot of app suggestions, and you can also search for apps. When you have selected an app, select from your content in that app; *refer to* 12.1.7.

12.1.5.3.5 *Add a Channel*

Anyone in the team can add new channels for new conversations. To add a channel, click on the ellipsis at the team name and select 'Add channel'.

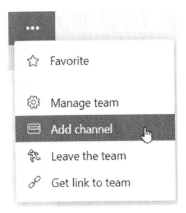

Give the channel a name and a description and click on 'Add'.

When you click on the ellipsis at the new channel, you may edit or delete the channel.

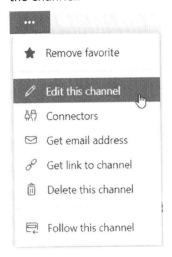

12.1.5.4   Private Chats

While team channels are conversations that all team members can see and join, the private chats are only visible to the person who started the chat and to those who have been invited to it.

When only one member is invited to a chat, there are four tabs in the main area and a plus sign for additional app content.

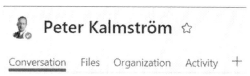

The 'Organization' tab gives information about the person you are chatting with – me, in this case – and the 'Activity' tab shows that person's other recent activities, for example in channel chats that you both have access to.

When there are several people in the chat, only the 'Conversation' and the 'Files' tabs are available.

The 'Conversation' tab is default and shows the ongoing chat in the same way as for Channel conversations.

The 'Files' tab shows files that have been shared in the chat. Files that were uploaded in private chats are not stored in a SharePoint library but in a folder called 'Microsoft Teams Chat Files' in the OneDrive for Business 'Files' library of the person who uploaded the file. From there, it is automatically shared with the people who participates in the private chat.

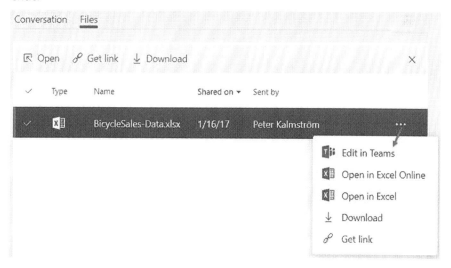

12.1.5.4.1 *Open a Private Chat*

189

Click on the Chat entry in the left pane. Now the middle pane will display all your recent private chats and chats that you have added to your Favorites. Click on one of the chats to open it again in the main area.

If enabled by the administrator, there is also a T-Bot chat where you can ask questions how to use Teams to a robot.

12.1.5.4.2 *Start a Private Chat*

To start a new private chat, click on the chat icon to the left of the search field, above the middle area.

A 'To' box is displayed on top of the main area. Start writing the name of a person or group you want to chat with, and select the correct option from the suggestions. Continue with the next person/group you want to invite. These people don't have to be team members. You can invite anyone in the organization, but no more than 10 people can participate in a private chat.

People who are added to a chat will get an e-mail message about it.

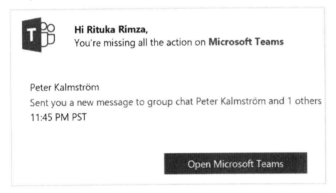

You can add more people to a private chat, but that will start a new chat with the included people, so the person or group who was added later will only see chat messages that are written after they have been invited.

Add more people by clicking on the icon far to the right on top of the main area.

12.1.5.4.3 *Video and Audio Calls*

The other two icons in the top right corner, *see* image above, are for video and audio calls. Use them to contact everyone who has been invited to the private chat.

If you only want to talk to one of the people, hover the mouse over the person's name on top of the main area and then on the icons.

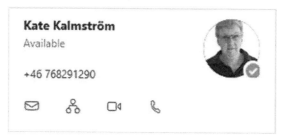

You can also send an e-mail and view the person's organization details.

12.1.5.4.4 *Name Private Chats*

To keep track of your private chats, you can name them, either when you create them or later.

To name the chat at creation, click on the arrow in the right end of the invitation box (1). This will open a naming box above the invitation box (2).

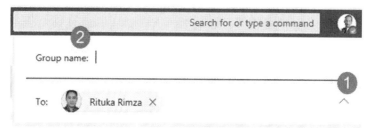

You can also name or rename a chat you initiated at a later stage, by clicking on the edit icon in the invitation box.

12.1.5.4.5 *Chat Options*

When you hover the mouse over a chat in the middle pane, an ellipsis will be visible. It gives three options.

Select 'Mute' if you want to stop getting notifications for the chat. A mute icon in the invitation box and at the chat entry in the middle pane will show that the chat has been muted. Open the ellipsis and select 'Unmute' to get notifications again.

The 'Hide' option removes the chat from the list in the middle pane. Use the search, *refer to* 12.1.8, to see it again.

12.1.6 *Meetings*

Video conversations (in Teams called "Meetings") can be started from chats, by clicking on the meetings icon under the chat box in channels.

Private chats have the icon in the top right corner, see above.

Other team or chat members can see that a meeting has started, so that they can join it if they so wish, and you can invite members by clicking on their names.

During the meeting, it is possible to switch between showing peoples photos and sharing your desktop or other content.

12.1.6.1 Schedule a Meeting

Video conversations can be scheduled in advance.

In the meeting dialog you can select the time and channel for the meeting, type details about the meeting and invite people. All team members can join via the 'Join' button at the meeting, *see* the image above.

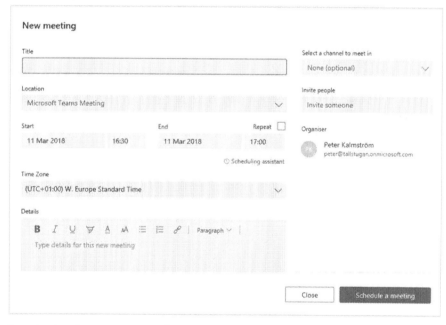

In private chats, you can also schedule a meeting from the compose box.

The Meeting dialog looks the same, but the current chat members are added automatically.

12.1.7 Connectors

Teams will get really useful if you connect content from other apps to the channels. These apps will be reached via additional tabs above the main area; *refer to* 12.1.5.3.4.

Click on the plus sign to the right of the existing tabs, to see a suggestion of apps, whose content can be added to the channel you have selected.

As you see from the image below, several other Office 365 apps and services can be added to Teams. Click on the icon for the app you want to use.

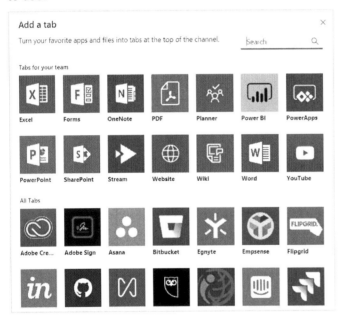

A new dialog will open, where all content you have access to from the selected app will be displayed.

Give the new tab a suitable name. Do not use the name of the connector, as suggested. As the tab shows one item – an Office file, a powerapp, a Power BI report – it is better to name the tab after that item. Then you can add and easily find multiple items of the same kind.

Should you want to rename or remove the tab, click on the arrow at the tab name. When this is written, only the Wiki tab and the tabs added by members can be renamed or removed.

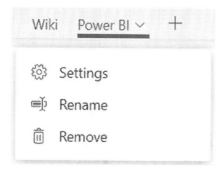

The 'Settings' link makes it possible to add a new file of the same type under the tab.

12.1.7.1   Connect a Powerapp

When you select PowerApps for a new tab in a channel, your own apps wIll be shown by default. Click on one of them to add it under the new tab. You can also select to show all apps or sample apps, or search for a suitable app.

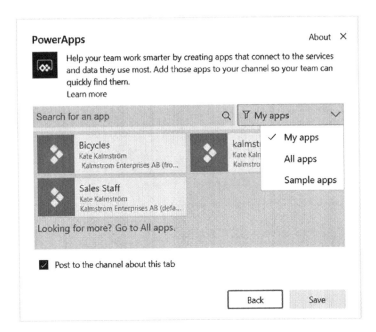

12.1.7.2 Connect Office Apps

When you select an Office app, you can add documents from the Files library, so that you have quick access to them. They can also be edited and downloaded directly under the tab.

12.1.7.3 Connect Planner

When you add a Planner tab to a Teams channel, you can see and work with plans in Teams. Plans that are created in Teams will show up in Planner and vice versa.

12.1.7.4 Connect Forms

When you connect Microsoft Forms, *refer to* chapter 17, to Teams, you can create a form or quiz that everyone in your team can see and edit. If you've already created a form in Forms, you can still add it to the tab to collect and show responses.

12.1.7.5 Connect Website

You can also add a secure website (starting with https://) to a Teams channel.

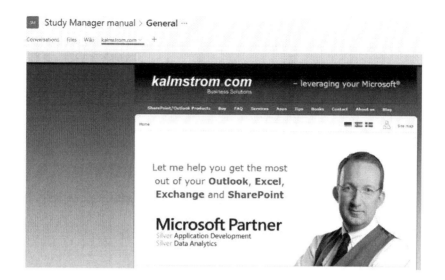

12.1.8 Search Teams

Teams has a search box on top of the main area. Hits are shown under the tabs Messages, People and Files, and they can be filtered in various ways to limit the search.

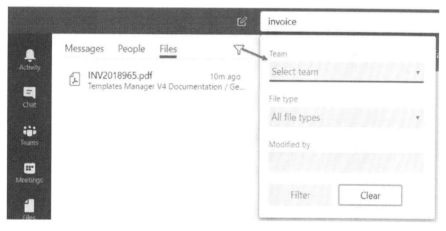

Currently private chat content do not show up in the search, but Microsoft investigates if this should be changed so that people can request to join them. Therefore, team owners should make sure that the team name and description do not include sensitive information.

Demo:

https://www.kalmstrom.com/Tips/Office-365-Course/Teams.htm

12.2 YAMMER

With Yammer, organizations can communicate, share files and work together in project or topic groups, just like you can in Teams. But Yammer is really the only app in Office 365 that allows you to have a conversation with the entire company, at least if the company is of considerable size.

Yammer is also great for structures that go beyond project timelines, such as building communities for skills and expertise development and communicating across all levels of an organization.

Yammer has a desktop app and also apps for Android, iOS and Windows Phone.

12.2.1 The Yammer Site

When you click on the Yammer icon in the Office 365 App Launcher or at office.com, you will be directed to the Yammer home page at https://www.yammer.com/.

The first time you set up a Yammer network, you will see a start page that is different from how it looks later. Only the left pane is the same. The rest of the page shows links to various settings, a checklist for what you, as the first administrator, should do and a download button for the Yammer desktop app.

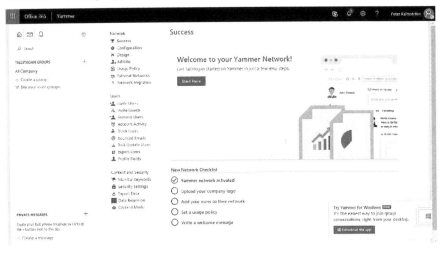

When other users join Yammer, they will see a different layout. The site now has a left pane and a right pane and a main conversation area in the middle.

198

12.2.1.1　Left Pane

The Yammer left pane has controls that decide what should be displayed in the main area.

In the upper part of the left pane there is an icon for an inbox, where you can see all chat messages you have received or sent, both private and in group conversations.

There is also alert icon for information about pending membership requests, additions to groups and similar, and a settings gear that I will describe later in this chapter.

The most important part of the left pane is the group section, which has links to all Yammer groups the current user is a member of or has requested access to. (See all groups by clicking on 'Discover more groups'.)

At the bottom of the left pane you can open private chat messages or create new ones.

12.2.1.2　The Right Pane

The right pane looks different depending on what is selected in the left pane and thereby shown in the main area.

- When private messages or the settings have been selected in the left pane, there is no right pane but just a main area.

- When the Yammer home page is selected, there is general Yammer info, suggested apps, groups and people and an invitation button.

  There is also a "Get started" box on top, that will have fewer suggestion as users become more engaged in Yammer.

- When a Yammer group has been selected in the left pane, the right pane holds info about that group. All group members can view and add group members and see statistics about group activity.

In the right pane of each group except the 'All company' group, members can also add files, links or related groups and select to subscribe or post by e-mail. There is also an embed code for the group feed.

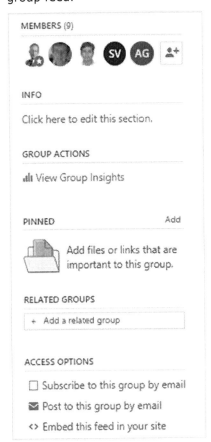

12.2.1.2.1 *Right Pane with Office 365 Group Connection*

When the Yammer group is connected to an Office 365 Group, *refer to* 12.2.5.3, the right pane also has links to the special Office 365 Group resources.

OFFICE 365 RESOURCES

▯ SharePoint document library

▯ SharePoint site

▯ OneNote

▯ Planner

12.2.2 Start Using Yammer

The easiest way for an administrator to set up Yammer for the tenant is to open the Office 365 Admin center and find the 'Yammer' entry under 'Admin centers'.

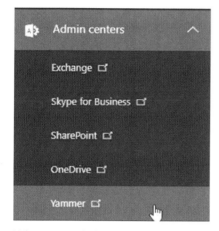

When you click on 'Yammer' you will be directed to the Network Admin settings for your tenant's Yammer. You can also reach these settings anyway from the settings gear in the top right corner of the Yammer left pane; *see* the arrow in the image below.

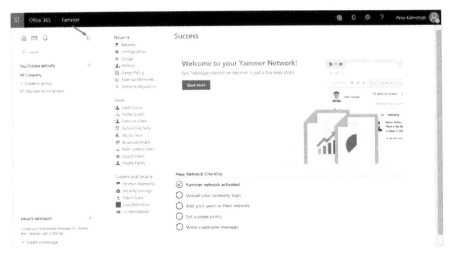

The Network Admin settings opens in the Success page, which gives a step by step guide to the Yammer setup.

12.2.2.1 Invite users

I recommend that you invite everyone in the tenant to the default 'All Company' group. This is easily done, as you can send invitation e-mails to all users at the same time by importing them from an address book or a CSV file.

Use the invite link 'Add your users to their network' on the Success page, or click on 'Invite Users' in the 'Users' group in the Network settings.

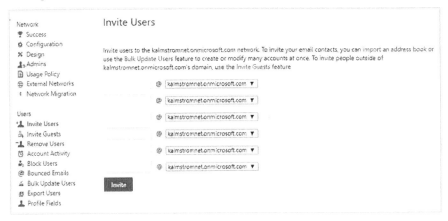

An e-mail invitation is sent to all who are invited. It has a 'Go to Yammer' button and a link to get the Yammer mobile app.

Welcome to Yammer, Stina!

You're now a part of kdemo13's private, social collaboration network. Yammer makes it easy to work together in teams and stay up to date on what others are working on.

Go to Yammer

Get the
mobile   Get the mobile app to catch
app:

When the user clicks on the button, he or she is directed to a page where user information should be added; *refer to* 12.2.8.1. Then the new user can see and send messages, create and join new groups, see, upload and edit files, chat with colleagues and do everything that regular users are allowed to.

12.2.3 Internal Network

The most used network in Yammer is the internal, or home network, where people within a tenant can connect and collaborate. Messages posted within your internal network are owned by your organization and cannot be shared externally.

In an external network, you can connect and collaborate with customers, suppliers and other contacts outside the tenant. The external networks can include users who have different e-mail domains.

12.2.3.1   Add Members to an Internal Network

The network admin can invite people to Yammer when the network is set up; *see* above. Later all members can invite people within the organization to the network by clicking on the invitation button in the right pane of the Yammer home page.

INVITE YOUR COWORKERS

Yammer works best when
your team is here too.

Invite them now

Now the main area will show the two options to invite new members, by e-mail address or by importing from an address book.

203

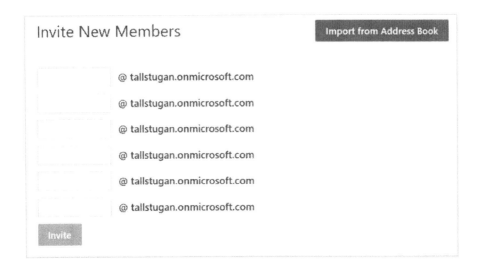

12.2.4 External Network

To create a new external network, click on 'Create a New Network' under the settings gear at the top right part of the left pane.

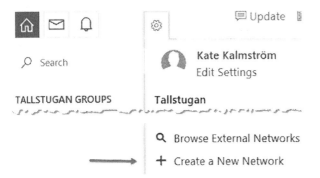

The dialog that opens has important permission options. By default the network is open, which means that all members can invite new members. If you want more control, select the 'Closed' option, which only allows network admins to invite new members.

You can also allow members of your internal network to join the external network without an invitation.

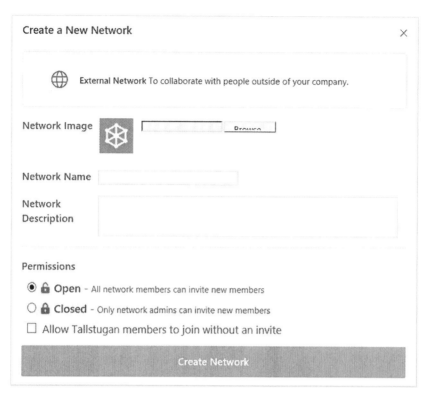

When you click on 'Create Network' a new network home page will open. It looks as the internal network home page, but the 'All Company' group is now called 'All Network'.

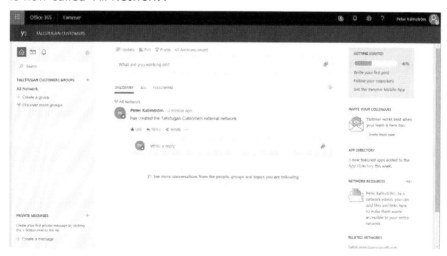

Now you can start inviting members to the external network.

205

Invite New Members

Import from Address Book

Yammer will send each person above an invite asking them to join this network.

12.2.5 Groups

Within a network, you can create groups of people who work with a certain project, who have a common interest or expertise etc.

When the Yammer group is public, which is default, everyone in the network can join and participate, without approval from an administrator.

Private groups require an invitation or approval from a group administrator, and they can be hidden from the Yammer group directory.

Just like networks, groups can be internal, with people only from the tenant, or external, including people from outside the tenant.

12.2.5.1   Create a Yammer Group

All users can create a Yammer group – which does not mean that everyone should do it! Before you create a group, consider if a Yammer group is the best option for your purpose, and if you are prepared to manage it.

To create a new group, click on the link '+ Create a new group' in the left pane. You can also use the plus sign to the right of the network name in the left pane.

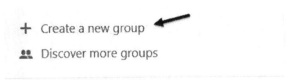

You can create an internal (default) or external group. Give it a name and add members.

Note that the default access value is Public, which means that anyone in the organization can view and participate in conversations.

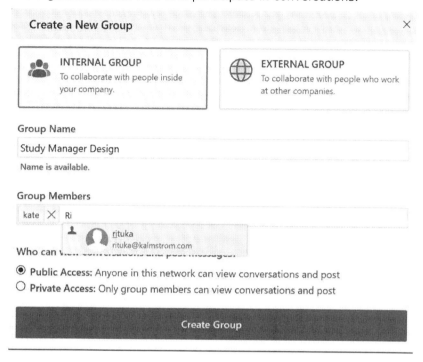

12.2.5.2   Group Settings

When the group has been created, you can add a description and an image for it via the 'Click here' link or the settings gear in the group banner on top of the main area.

When you have added the description, it will be visible instead of the 'Click here' text.

In the group settings, you can also manage members and add new members.

12.2.5.3   Office 365 Groups

Microsoft is currently rolling out a connection between Yammer groups and Office 365 Groups. This means that both new and existing Yammer will be connected to Office 365 and get the Office 365 Group resources; *refer to* chapter 9.

The new feature only applies to internal, public and private, listed Yammer groups. External users cannot be added.

It also only applies to Office 365 tenants that are associated with one single Yammer network. Additionally, Office 365 Identity must be enforced under Network Admin >Security Settings in Yammer.

12.2.6 Members

Yammer participants can be network administrators, group administrators or members. One person can of course have different roles in different contexts. A network administrator can for example be the group administrator of one group and a member of another group.

The person who starts the Yammer network will automatically become the network administrator, but more people can be appointed. Network admins can delete content, remove members, invite guest users and configure security settings.

The person who creates a group will become group administrator. The group admin have the same privileges over that group as the network admins have over the whole network. The group admin can appoint more people group admins, *see* below

12.2.6.1 Add Members to a Group

The Yammer members will be automatically added to the 'All company' group. To join other groups they must either join manually (public groups), request access or be invited (private groups).

Members can be added to a group when the group is created; *refer to* 12.2.2.1.

To add members to a group after the creation, the group admin can select the group in the left pane and then click on the plus icon in the top part of the right pane.

The member to the left in the image above is me, and the star on my profile picture indicates that I am the group admin.

In the dialog that opens, you can search for people and invite new members. You can also see the current members and remove them or make them admins.

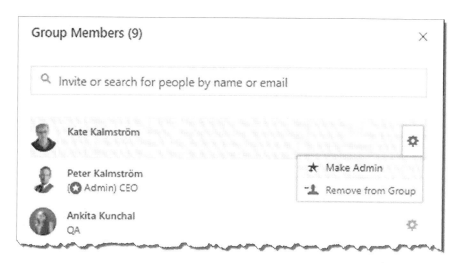

In the group settings, you can also manage members and add new members from the global address list; *refer to* 12.2.5.2.

12.2.7 Conversations

The most important part of Yammer is of course the conversations, and most of the activity in Yammer takes place in these conversations. Each group has a chat, but there is also a possibility to send and receive private chat messages. Both are displayed in the main area.

12.2.7.1 Group Chats

When you click on a group name in the left pane, the chat for that group is shown in the main area. All group members can see and write in the group chat. The 'All Company' chat is open for all.

All conversations are displayed by default, but you can also select to see only new conversations. Make this selection in the head banner, where you also can reach the files that have been added to the group and search the group content.

When a new member has joined the network or a group, there will be an auto-generated message about it in that network's or group's conversation.

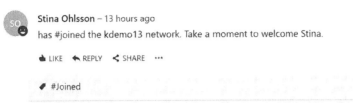

Stina Ohlsson – 13 hours ago

has #joined the kdemo13 network. Take a moment to welcome Stina.

👍 LIKE   🔙 REPLY   ◀ SHARE   ⋯

🔖 #Joined

Peter Kalmström replying to Stina Ohlsson: ✕

Welcome to Yammer, Stina   📎

SO Stina Ohlsson

Notify additional people..

Post

Messages can be liked and shared to other conversations or as a private message. Use the 'REPLY' button to open a compose box when there is no empty compose box below the message you want to answer.

👍 LIKE   🔙 REPLY   ◀ SHARE   ⋯

If there is a box, you can just start writing.

Under the ellipsis to the right of 'SHARE' there are more options.

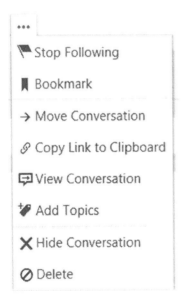

Files can be added to messages, and you can open a preview of the file directly in the message.

In your own posted messages, there is also a possibility to edit the message. When a message has been edited it is marked with 'Edited' after the date. Click on 'Edited' to see earlier versions of the message.

In the bottom right corner of the chat box, there are possibilities to search for and add an animated .gif and to add files from SharePoint, Yammer or your computer.

Yammer has however not (yet) an option to start a video conversation, as in Teams. The formatting possibilities are also more limited than in Teams.

Above the chat fields there are more options to categorize the entry if you don't want to use the default 'Update' option. The compose boxes look a bit different if you select to create a poll or give praise. The announcement box gives some formatting options.

■ Update   🖾 Poll   🏆 Praise   ◀ Announcement

Company Outing   📎

| B | I | ≔ | ≔ | 🔗 | 🔗 |

Next Friday we will have an outing to Öland for the whole company. More info soon!

12.2.7.2   Private chats

Private chats are created from a link or a plus sign at the bottom of the left pane. Above the link, the latest chat messages that you follow are listed.

The plus and the link opens the same chat message dialog. Start writing to have suggestions on receivers.

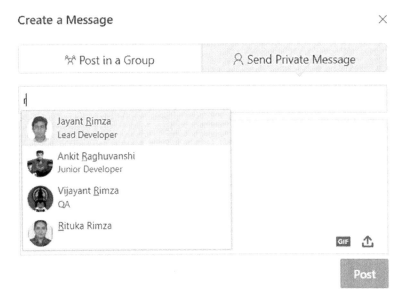

The private message is default, but you can also select 'Post in a Group' and have a selection of all groups you are a member of.

When you send a private message, the receiver will have a notification at the inbox icon in the left pane.

Both the sender and the receiver will be following the message automatically. Stop following it to remove it from the left pane and the inbox.

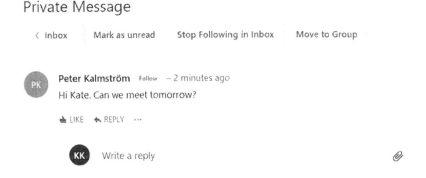

12.2.8 Yammer Member Options

To some extent, Yammer users can influence the content and look of the Yammer groups they are members of. Under the settings gear in the left pane, regular members have multiple options.

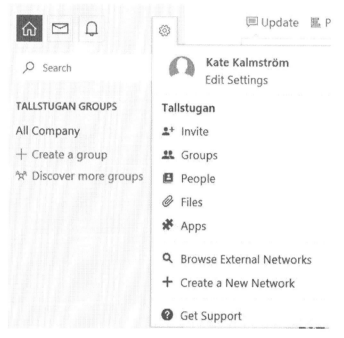

Use 'Invite' when you want to invite people within your organization to Yammer. All invited people will have an e-mail where they can accept the invitation.

'Groups' will show all groups in the main area. Each group tile has a 'Join' or a 'Joined' button. Click on the '+ Join' button to join a public group at once or ask permission to join a private group. The 'Joined' text will change into 'Leave' when you hover the mouse over it.

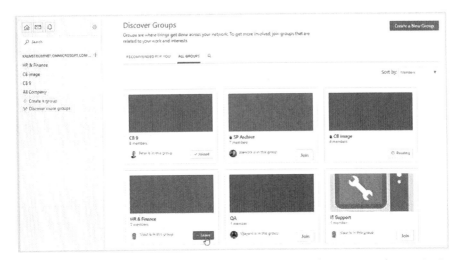

When you select 'People' you will see all the tenant's users and can start following or send private chat messages to them. The chat window will pop up in the bottom right corner. It is a regular chat where you can send files and invite more people but without the extra features that you can find in the Teams chat.

For 'Files' *refer to* 12.2.9 below.

'Apps' give suggestions on apps that you can connect to Yammer.

12.2.8.1 Member Settings

All members can – and should – fill out information about themselves in the member settings. You can reach them from under the settings gear in the top right corner of the left pane.

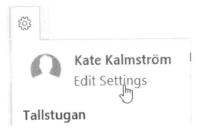

In the main area, you will now see all your profile settings. They are arranged under various tabs.

Profile

Basics

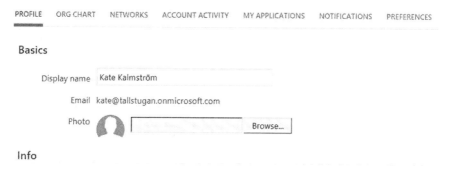

Display name   Kate Kalmström

Email   kate@tallstugan.onmicrosoft.com

Photo   Browse...

Info

12.2.9 Files

In Yammer you can upload and see files in conversations and private chats. Files can also be reached from and uploaded to group directories and a personal directory:

- Open any group and click on the 'FILES' tab in the banner. This shows a list of files that are associated with that group. The files can be sorted by file type.

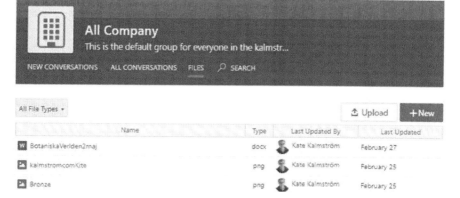

- Here you can also create new Office files and edit files.

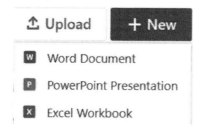

- Groups that are associated with an Office 365 group also have a Files library in SharePoint; *refer to* 9.5.2.1. In the long term, Microsoft is planning to store all Yammer files in SharePoint.

- The 'Files' option under the top left ellipsis, *see* 12.2.8 above, opens a personal files directory where you can find all files you have access to, from all groups you are a member of.

- When you upload a file here, it will be added to the 'All Company' group.

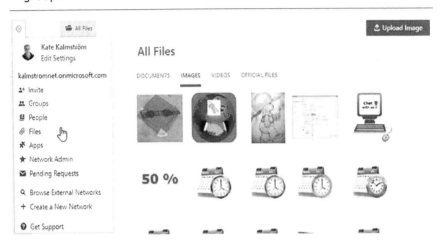

12.2.9.1 Preview in Conversations

When you click on a file that has been uploaded directly to a conversation, it will open in preview mode in that conversation and give options to Share, Download and Go to File.

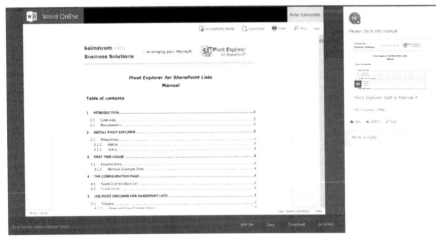

For Office files there is also an edit option that opens the file in the Online edition of the Office app, but it is only for quick changes. For more elaborate editing I recommend to open the file in a directory instead, *see* next section below.

12.2.9.2   Rich File View

When you click on a file in a Files directory, it will open in rich file view, a page that's dedicated to a specific file. If the file was uploaded in a conversation, this chat will open below the preview window.

A new conversation will open if the file was uploaded directly via the 'Upload file' button so that there are no earlier messages in the feed.

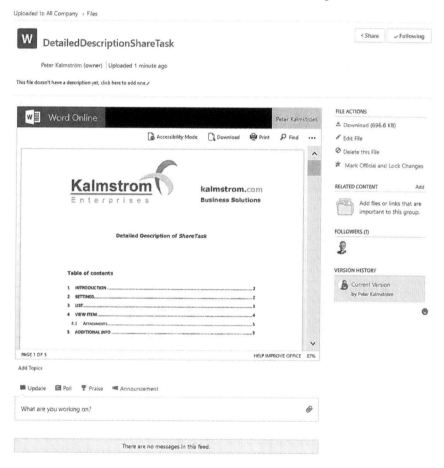

In the right pane of the rich file view page, you can perform various 'FILE ACTIONS' from the right pane. This section looks a bit different depending on if the file is an Office file or not. Office files can be edited directly from Yammer and saved back, so there is no need to upload a new version.

For other files you can upload a new version that replaces the old one.

FILE ACTIONS

↧ Download (4.8 MB)

↗ View Fullscreen

✎ Edit File

⊘ Delete this File

★ Mark Official and Lock Changes

FILE ACTIONS

↧ Download (780.2 KB)

⬆ Upload a New Version

↗ View Fullscreen

⊘ Delete this File

★ Mark Official and Lock Changes

Only administrators and file owners can delete files. When no more changes should be allowed, the administrator can mark the file as Official and lock it. It will then be locked for editing or replacement by all users except the admin and the owner.

12.2.9.3   Follow File

When you follow a file, you subscribe to conversations that reference that file, and when a new version of the file is available, you will receive a notification. When you upload a file to Yammer you will follow it automatically.

If you want to follow a file that you have not uploaded yourself, click on the '+Follow' button in the Rick File View, at the 'Share' button.

12.2.10   Share

A public group's conversation messages and files can be shared to people who are not members of the group and therefore normally should not see them.

12.2.10.1 Share a message

To share a message from a conversation, click on the 'SHARE' button below the message.

A dialog will open, where you can select whether you want to post the message in another group or as a private message. You can add a file and give a comment, and there is also a link to the full conversation.

218

When you select to share the message with a group, you will have a choice of groups. When you select to share the message in a private chat, you will have a choice of people.

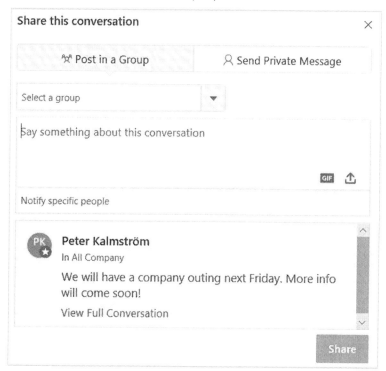

12.2.10.2 Share a File

Open the file you want to share and click on the Share button in the top right corner of the rich file view, next to the Follow/Following button.

The dialog that opens gives the same options as when you share a message, *see* image above, except 'View Full Conversation'.

12.2.11 *Admin Options*

The Yammer Network Administrator has many options at hand that are not available for other users.

The right pane of the Yammer home page and the 'All Company' group has a 'Company Resources' group. Here network admins can add files and links that the network should have easy at hand.

COMPANY RESOURCES   Add

 Peter Kalmström, as a
network admin, you can
add files and links here
to make them easily
accessible to your entire
network.

Files can be added from the Yammer file directories, and if there is a
connection to Office 365 Groups they can also be fetched from the
group's SharePoint document library.

Links to secure websites can also be added. This is how it might look:

COMPANY RESOURCES   Add

🔗 The kalmstrom.com website

W Guidelines for image mani...

W Handle New Subscriber

Most of the Network Admin options are however found in the network
settings page. Click on the settings wheel in the top right corner of the
left pane to reach them. Then select 'Network Admin'.

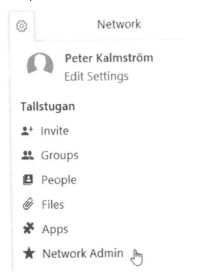

The Admin settings give many options for network, user, content and security management. I will not go into all options here, but in the image below you can see the Export Data feature.

12.2.11.1 Export Data

Yammer gives a possibility to export Yammer data. Select Export Data in the Network settings to package and export all messages, notes, files, topics, users and groups to a .zip file. This file contains separate .csv files for messages, users, topics and groups and folders for files and pages.

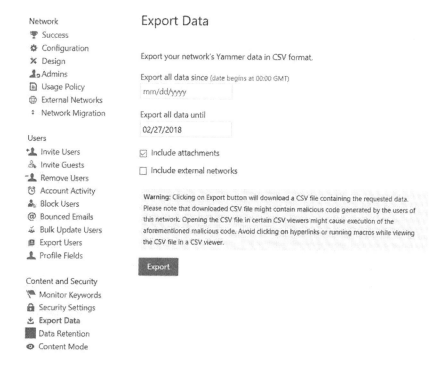

There is no similar export option in Teams, and this difference between the two conversation apps might be important for some organizations.

12.2.12   SharePoint Connection

Yammer conversations can be added to SharePoint pages.

In modern pages, *refer to* 6.3.2, you can add a web part that displays the Yammer feed. Search for the group you want to show in the web part settings.

A feed for all groups but 'All Company' can also be embedded in a SharePoint wiki page. You can find the embed code at the bottom of the right pane in Yammer.

12.2.13   Delve Connection

Each file card on the Delve home page, *refer to* chapter 7, has the option to start a Yammer conversation about the file. In that case, a Yammer conversation is opened in the Delve right pane.

12.3   Summary

In the chapter about the Teams and Yammer conversation apps, I have described how teams and Yammer groups can be created and managed. We have looked at how these apps handle private chats and chats for teams and groups and how files and other apps can be used.

We have also looked at the meeting feature in Teams and the Yammer external networks, and we have discussed the options given by the connected Office 365 Group apps. Teams is strongly connected to Office 365 Groups, while Yammer still only has this possibility in certain cases.

Both these conversation apps are useful and will surely evolve more in the future. I hope this chapter has given you a good overview over their current features, so that you in each case can judge if Teams or Yammer is the best choice for your organization.

13 STAFFHUB

Microsoft StaffHub is intended to help users who don't work at a desk to manage their workday, and to make it easy for managers to schedule work and share information.

The typical scenario for StaffHub usage is that managers access the service via their computers and handle scheduling and send out information, while workers use their mobile devices to see schedules and send and receive messages.

13.1 STAFFHUB AND GROUPS

When a StaffHub team is created, *see* below, an Office 365 Group for that team is created automatically. However, so far that group is not used much in StaffHub. All the Office 365 Group resources are found in the user mailboxes, but only the file sharing is present in the StaffHub itself. Even if there is a shared calendar, StaffHub does not store schedule information in it.

When we talk about a "group" in StaffHub, we actually most often refer to a section of a team, which Microsoft also has decided to call a group. You can learn more about such groups in 13.4.2, and when there can be a doubt I always write either "Office 365 Group" or "StaffHub group".

13.2 FIRST TIME ADMIN USAGE

When you click on the StaffHub tile in the Office 365 App Launcher or at office.com, you will be directed to https://staffhub.office.com. (This link is mainly used by managers, because other users access StaffHub via apps in their tablets or mobile phones.)

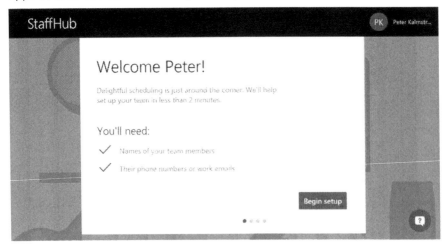

The first time a new user opens the StaffHub site, he/she is asked to create a team:

1. Click on 'Begin setup'.

2. Give the team a name. The team can for example be people working in a shop, on a construction site or at a restaurant, and in that case it is suitable to give the name of the shop/site/restaurant. Click on 'Create team'.

3. Confirm or change the time zone.

4. (Give your mobile number, to send yourself a link to the mobile app.)

5. Enter names and contact details for the staff. All users need to have Office 365 accounts, and you will have suggestions to select from when you start writing. When you select a name, the e-mail address and phone number will be added automatically.

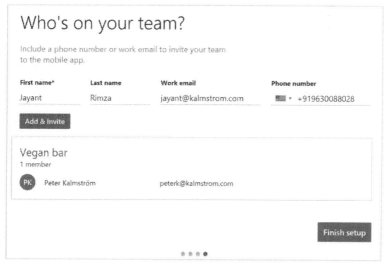

6. When you click on 'Add & Invite' an e-mail or SMS message with a link will be sent to the users, so that they can download the mobile app.

7. Click on 'Finish setup' when everyone has been added. Should you need to add more users or remove people from the team later, you can do that later in the schedule page, *see* 13.3 below.

Now when you have built a team, a corresponding Office 365 Group has been created.

13.3 PERMISSIONS

A user who creates a StaffHub team will be the manager of that team. All other users will have 'Read only' permission over the StaffHub content.

These two permission levels are the only ones that exist in StaffHub. The manager can allow more people to create or modify schedules under the 'Team' tab in the command bar on the Manager's home page.

13.4 MANAGER

We will first have a look at how the manager of StaffHub works with scheduling and management of team members and groups.

13.4.1 Schedule

When the setup has been finished, you will see an empty scheduling calendar. Now you can arrange the staff in groups and start working on their shifts.

13.4.1.1 Shifts

To add a new shift, click on the ellipsis in the bottom right corner of the time slot you want to add a shift to, and select an option.

The easiest way is of course to select and copy a range of shifts from one team member and paste it in for another member. Copy and paste with Crtl+C and Ctrl+V works also.

When you select or 'Add shift', a right pane opens where you can select hours, color code and add notes and activities.

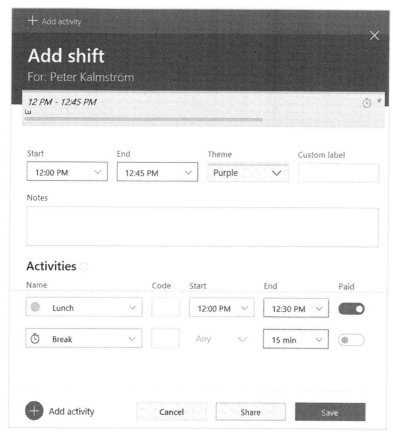

You can select to Share the shift at once or to save it and share it later.

When you select 'Add time off' another right pane will open.

Sometimes shift schedules remain similar over time, and then you can copy an entire week instead of adding new shifts. The 'Copy last week' button is placed to left above the actual schedule, and here you can also find a button that prints the schedule.

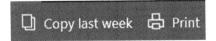

13.4.1.2   Day Notes

On top of the shifts for each day, there is room for messages about special events during the day that the staff should be aware of – or anything else you want to use the space for!

⏱ 81.5 Hrs	16 Hrs	17 Hrs	17 Hrs
Day notes	Wedding party at 3	Visit from HQ	Add new note

13.4.1.3   Views

You can see the calendar by Day, Week, Month. When you have set the time span (to the right above the schedule), you can select to view that spam in various ways by combining the icons to the right.

Below is part of the default view. It shows all people (the first icon is active) and all groups (the icon to the right). Their work hours are marked in bold text.

When the middle icon is combined with the right icon, the schedule shows how many are working in each group each day in the selected period.

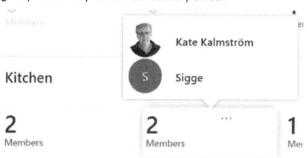

When you click again on the right icon, the group separation disappears.

13.4.2 Groups

A StaffHub group is a part of the team, for example waiters or cooks in a restaurant team. By default the team members are placed in two groups with the manager in one group and the other users in another group.

13.4.2.1   Rename and Remove Group

The "other users" group is by default called "New Group", but you should of course rename it to something more fitting. Do that by clicking on the group name. (Here is also where you delete the group.)

New Group   ✕

13.4.2.2   Add Group

You can add more StaffHub groups by clicking on 'Add group' below the existing groups.

 Add Group

13.4.2.3   Remove Group

To the right of the group name, at the other end of the schedule, there are three icons. Use the basket to delete the group.

13.4.2.4   Reorder Groups

To change the order of the StaffHub groups, click on the middle icon to the far right of the group name, *see* image above. A right pane will open, where you can drag and drop the groups to reorder them.

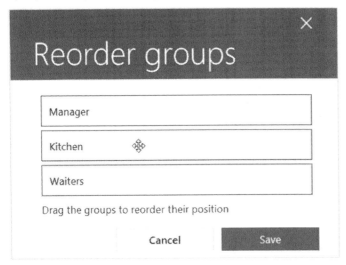

13.4.3 Members

Member contacts and permissions can be managed under the 'Team' tab.

13.4.3.1 Add Members to Groups

Add members to a StaffHub group by clicking on the add member icon in the default calendar view, to the far right of the group name.

A right pane will open. Start writing a name and an e-mail address, and select the correct suggestion. Add a mobile number or e-mail address and select if the new member should have manager rights. This setting is off by default. Save and invite the new member, and an invitation will be sent.

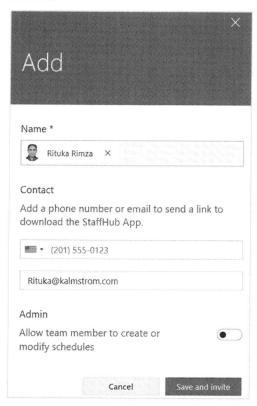

13.4.3.2 Remove or Move Member

To remove a team member from a StaffHub group, or move a member up or down in the same group, click on the ellipsis in the bottom right corner of the name box and select an option.

⟐ Move team member

·· ✕ Remove from group

13.4.4 Share

When the schedule is good, click on the 'Share with team' button to the
left above the schedule. Now all users will see the schedule in their
mobile devices.

You are asked to confirm schedule range in a right pane – by default the
range is same as the view. You can also opt to only share the schedule
with affected members.

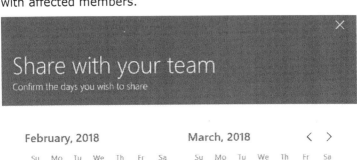

13.4.4.1 Files

Under the 'Files' tab, you can add files and links that are useful to the staff, for example guidelines and demonstrations. As StaffHub builds on Office 365 Groups, the files are actually stored in the SharePoint 'Documents' library for the corresponding group.

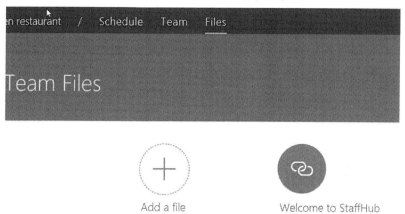

13.4.5 Settings

The StaffHub settings are reached from the settings gear in the right part of the command bar.

In the settings you can edit team information and schedule start of the week day. Click on the icon at a request reason to change it. You can also add more reasons.

233

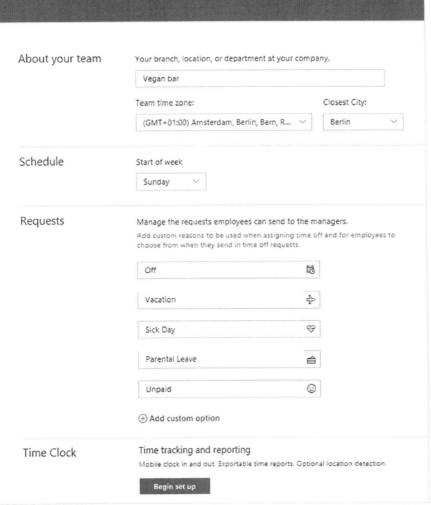

The settings is also the place where you delete the team. This is done in the top left corner of the page.

13.4.5.1 Time Clock

If you want users to be able to clock in and out in their mobiles, you should turn on the Time Clock. Location can also be added.

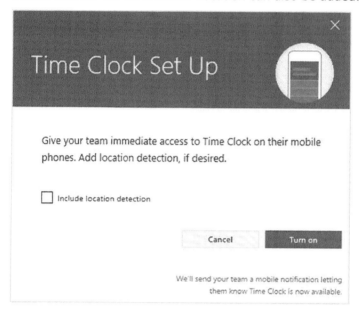

When the Time Clock has been turned on, there is a new 'Export' button in the settings. Click on it to open or download an Excel file with working time related information about each team member.

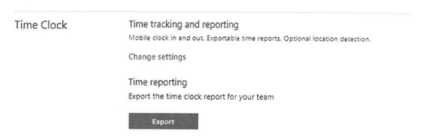

When the Time Clock is turned on, users will have a Time Clock button and a status circle in their mobile devices.

13.5   MOBILE APPS

Team members who are not managers, use StaffHub in their mobile apps, and currently the Android and iOS operating systems are supported.

The users can see the schedule in different views in a mobile friendly interface and use the app to check or change their shifts, ask for leaves and get information from managers – but also to communicate with colleagues. The manager can of course also communicate with team members via the mobile app.

The home screen of the StaffHub app gives a summary of upcoming shifts and shows notes for the day. Users can also see who else is working at the same time.

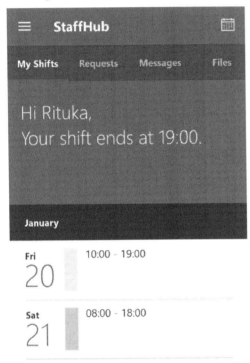

13.5.1 Swap Shifts

Via StaffHub, users can request to swap shifts with one another. When a team member finds another person that has a schedule that makes a swap possible, the request is formalized:

1. User 1 selects the Requests tab (a) and taps 'Swap Or Offer Shift' (b).

2.

Swap Or Offer Shift

Request Time Off

3. Under the 'Swap My Shift' tab, User 1 selects the shift to swap.

4. User 1 selects a shift of User 2 to work instead.

5. (User 1 types a reason for the swap request.)

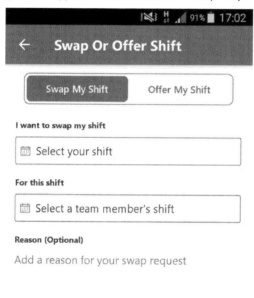

6. User 1 clicks on the 'Send Request' button.

7. User 2 receives and accepts or denies the swap request. (If the request is denied the process stops here.)

8. The accepted request goes to the manager for approval.

9. The manager taps on the request under the Requests tab.

10. The manager taps either 'Approve' or 'Deny'.

11. (The manager gives a reason.)

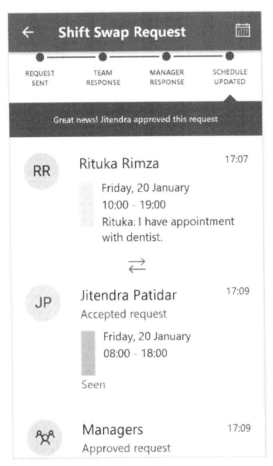

12. If the request has been approved, the schedule will be updated automatically.

Shift offers and time off requests can be sent and approved/denied in a similar way.

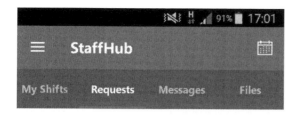

Need a schedule change?

You can request time off here or offer your shift to a coworker. Tap the plus button to start.

13.5.2 Chat

In the StaffHub chat, the staff can talk with each other and communicate with managers in the same app where they check schedules and access company resources.

Tap a colleague's contact icon to open a compose box. Now a chat message can be typed and sent.

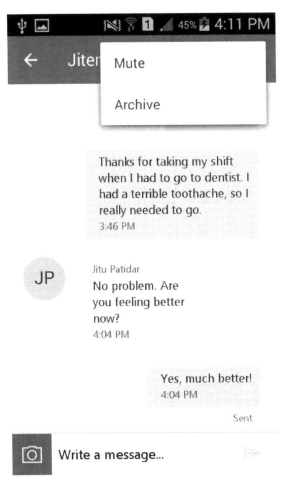

The chat supports private chats, group chats and file sharing. Images can be seen in a preview in the chat.

StaffHub currently has its own chat feature, but in the future Microsoft is planning to let the StaffHub messaging share the same backend as Teams.

13.6 ADMIN SETTINGS

Any user can create a StaffHub team and make a schedule, but some settings require administrator permissions. You can reach the StaffHub settings via the Office 365 Admin settings >Services & add-ins. When you open the StaffHub settings you will only see a link to https://staffhub.office.com/admin.

Here you can set StaffHub to create new Office 365 accounts for users who don't already have an account in the tenant. You can also add custom fields in the form that managers have to complete when they create a new team, such as "Location ID" or "Region", and enter links to important resources. The links will appear in the StaffHub mobile app, under Employee Resources.

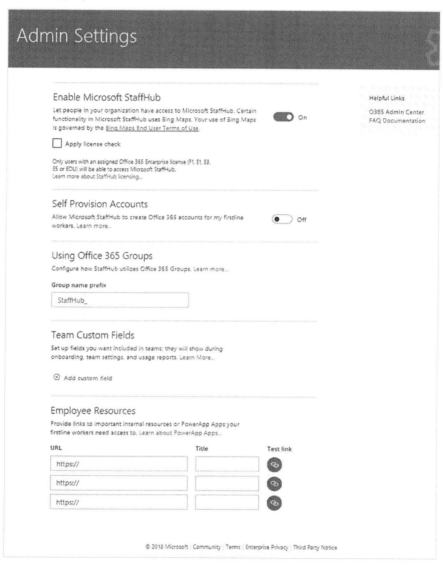

An announcement feature is included in Microsoft's plans for StaffHub. It will, if enabled in the Admin settings, allow certain people to send e-mail announcements to everyone who is using the StaffHub mobile app.

13.7 FLOW INTEGRATION

StaffHub is one of the services that can be used with Microsoft Flow; *refer to* 14.2. It is not (yet) possible to create flows directly from within StaffHub, but Flow has many options for automation of StaffHub processes, such as adding new shifts to a calendar or sending e-mails when a new schedule has been published.

13.8 SUMMARY

StaffHub is an interesting app for groups where the users don't work at a desktop and have a PC or laptop. And they are many!

StaffHub makes the scheduling easy for managers, and it is of course ideal to let users have everything in their smart devices and to formalize common processes like shift swaps and time off requests.

In this chapter we have looked at how managers can create a team and schedule work hours for its members, and we have also seen how other users can work with StaffHub in their mobiles.

14 FLOW AND POWERAPPS – AUTOMATION SERVICES

All business problems cannot be solved with off-the-shelf solutions, but developing custom solutions is often costly and time consuming. Flow and PowerApps are two Microsoft services that give people a possibility to solve at least smaller problems without having to bring in experts for custom software development.

Even if Flow and PowerApps aim to solve different problems, they have several technical similarities. I will start this chapter with these, before I go into first Flow and then PowerApps.

14.1 IN COMMON FOR FLOW AND POWERAPPS

Both Flow and PowerApps can integrate across multiple data sources and deliver across multiple devices, from desktop to mobile. That is one reason to bring them together in one chapter. Power BI, described in chapter 15, share this quality, but Flow and PowerApps have more in common that is not shared by Power BI:

- The Flow and PowerApps admin centers are connected.

- Data Policies can be set for both apps.

- SharePoint lists with the modern interface give a possibility to create flows and powerapps based on the list data directly from the list.

- Both Flow and PowerApps can be enhanced with extra features that are not included in the Office 365 subscription. These enhancements are bought as Plans, which contain extra environments and data sources for both apps.

- My recommendation to use special accounts is the same for both apps.

14.1.1 Plans

PowerApps is included in the Office 365 Enterprise, Business Premium and Essentials subscriptions. However, the Flow and PowerApps features included in the standard subscription can be enhanced with Plan1 and Plan2 subscriptions.

I will not go into the Plan enhancements here, because I think my readers first want to try the regular services before they start thinking about enhancements. All images below are taken from a standard Enterprise subscription with no extra Plan added.

However, some explanations are in place here, as some features that are only available in the plans are visible in both Flow and PowerApps even if they are not included in the subscription. It is even possible to start – deliberate or accidental – trials of these Plans from within Flow and PowerApps when you try to use not included features.

14.1.1.1   Environments

An environment is a space to store your organization's flows, powerapps, and business data. You can use them to separate flows and apps that have different roles, security requirements, or targets.

A single environment is automatically created for each tenant and shared by all users in that tenant. By default all users can create flows and powerapps in that environment.

With the Plan 2 enhancement, tenant administrators can create more environments in the Flow and PowerApps Admin centers. Using environments gives a performance benefit, but it also means that the flow or powerapp is limited to the resources of that environment.

14.1.1.2   Premium Connectors

Flow and PowerApps lets you connect to a wide range of online services. The Plans include even more services, called Premium connectors. In some views they are visible even though you cannot connect to them, and when you try, you are prompted to upgrade to a Plan.

14.1.2 Admin Centers

Both Flows and PowerApps have links to their admin centers in the Office 365 Admin center.

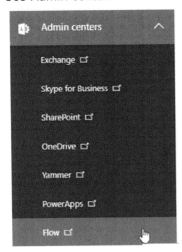

You will be directed to https://admin.flow.microsoft.com/ or https://admin.powerapps.microsoft.com/, depending on which link you choose, but any changes you make in the Flow Admin center will impact the PowerApps Admin center and vice versa. Therefore, these two can actually be considered as one Admin center for both services.

Without any Plan addition, you can not do much in this Admin center, but there are still some valuable features. You can download a CSV file with data about user licenses for both services, and you can also see how much of your Flow quota you have used. (The Office 365 subscription gives 2000 runs per month, which is enough for most flows. To have more, you must subscribe to a Plan.)

You can also set Data policies for the tenant in the Flow/PowerApps Admin center.

14.1.2.1   Data Policies

To prevent business data from being published to external services, such as social media sites, tenant admins can set Data Retention Policies in the Flow/PowerApps Admin center. Select 'Data Policies' in the left pane and click on 'New policy' in the top right corner.

There is a selection which environments the new policy should be applied to, but without an extra Plan you only have one environment and can only choose the first option, 'Apply to ALL environments'.

245

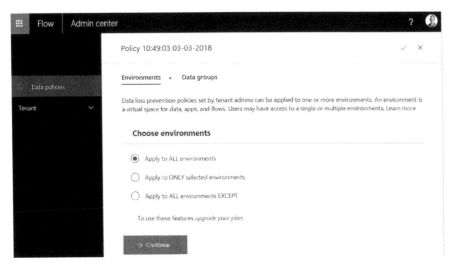

When you click on 'Continue', the 'Data groups' tab will open. Here you will see all available services and how they are grouped in 'Business data only' and 'No business data allowed'.

Data sources that contain business critical data, such as SharePoint and SQL, should go into the 'Business data only' group, while those that do not contain protected information would go to the 'No business data allowed' group. When you add a service to one of the data groups, it will automatically be removed from the other group.

Click on the plus sign in one of the groups to add services to that group. Click on 'Save Policy' when enough services have been added. Now users who create a powerapp or a flow will not be able to combine connections from both groups.

14.1.3 Storage

Flows and PowerApps are stored in the personal account of the user who created them (and in the region that hosts the environment of that user, if multiple environments are used). This might be good for personal apps, but it creates issues if a user who has created them for the organization leaves his/her position.

Therefore, any organization that decides to automate things with Flow and PowerApps, should make sure to create special user accounts for them. With dedicated accounts, the organization can continue using and editing the flows or powerapps even if a user leaves. You can also manage potential costs in cases of high volume flows or powerapps.

14.2   FLOW

Flow is a service for workflow creation, and when created in Flow, a workflow is often just called a "flow". Flows can be used for all kinds of SharePoint Online lists and libraries, and also for other cloud based services, to automate processes that need to be performed repeatedly.

Flows are often used for notification sending, but they can also calculate time, archive list items and perform many other tasks that would have been tedious and time consuming – or not performed at all – without a flow.

A flow is built with three components: trigger, condition(s) and action(s). You create the flow by combining these components in a way that gives the result you require.

Flows are intended to eventually replace SharePoint 2010 and SharePoint 2013 workflows. While workflows are limited to SharePoint sites, the flows can be used extensively with various services, and you can create flows for elaborate collaboration over multiple platforms.

Microsoft wants Flows to be a no-code, rapid application development environment, and as such it has certain limitations. I would still recommend a flow over a classic workflow – but use it with a special account, *see* above.

Here I will explain the basics of Flow and flow creation, and after that I will give some examples on how to create useful flows. Feel welcome to use my example flows, or parts of them, or to just study them to understand the flow creation process.

14.2.1 The Flow Site

When you click on the Flow tile in the Office 365 App Launcher or at office.com, you will be directed to the Flow home page at https://flow.microsoft.com.

From the Flow home page, you can create new flows, edit existing flows, connect to new services, search for flow templates and learn how to manage Flow.

At the bottom of the Flow home page, users can download the Flow mobile app.

14.2.2 Connect to Service

A flow is connected to at least one online service. Before you can start building a flow you must be connected to the included service(s).

Each Flow account can only have one connection to each service. The Office 365 subscription includes many services, and these are categorized as Standard. Connections that require a Plan subscription are called Premium.

14.2.2.1   Current Connections

Click on the Settings gear in the right part of the Office 365 navigation bar and select `Connections' to see existing connections and add more connections.

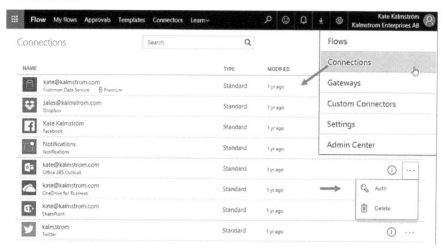

The info icon at each current connection gives information about that service, and under the ellipsis you can find links to authentication details and to delete the connection.

There is also a 'New connection' button to the right (hidden by the settings gear dropdown in the image above).

   New connection

Click on 'New connection', to see a list of unconnected services in alphabetical order. Only standard connectors are displayed here, if you have not paid the extra fee, of course. Click on the plus sign to add a connection.

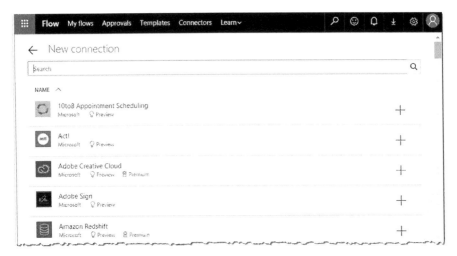

A dialog opens where you can allow the connection and enter your credentials. This dialog looks different for different services.

14.2.2.2   Search Connector

When you click on 'Connectors' in the top banner, you will see all available connectors, also Premium and custom connectors. You can filter by Standard connectors in the dropdown to the right of the search field on top. The search field is needed, because here the apps are not sorted alphabetically.

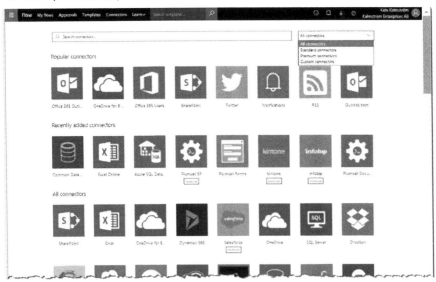

Click on one of the icons, and you will have more information about the service and a number of templates for it. In the image below, Twitter has been selected and templates that include Twitter are shown.

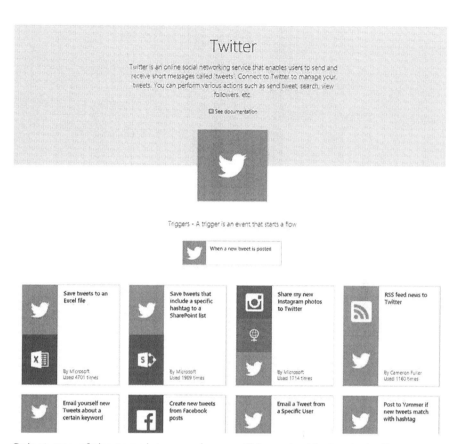

Select one of the templates, and you will be asked to log in to the service you are not yet logged in to. Then you can start working with your flow, using the service you just connected to.

14.2.3 Flow Creation Basics

When you create a flow, you always start with a template. There are many predefined templates to choose from, and there is also a blank template, if you want to start from scratch.

When you select the template for the flow, you also select the trigger. Therefore, what you do in the creation is to define parameters for the trigger and set condition(s) and action(s). An action often includes a

251

message, and in that case the receiver, subject and body text of that message is defined in the action part.

Flows are built in a flow builder with boxes where you select the right triggers, actions and conditions.

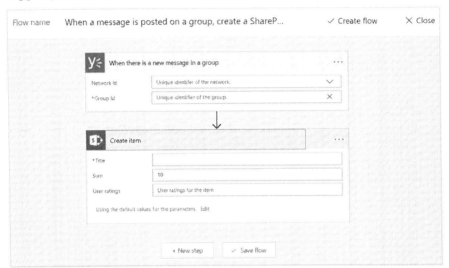

There are three ways to begin creating a flow, and the final is the same for all flows, but the steps in the flow builder vary with each flow.

14.2.3.1   Create from the Flow Site Home

At the Flow home page you can search for a template or use one of the suggested ones. If you want to create an approval flow, you can find approval templates under their own tab in the top banner.

The templates are sorted in groups, and if you click on the 'See more templates' below the templates that are shown by default, you will see all groups and all templates.

Within each group, the templates can be filtered by popularity, name or created date. There is also a search box.

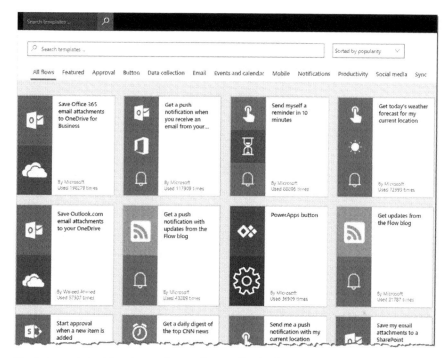

Each template tile shows icons that tell which services are involved in the flow and gives a short description of the trigger and what the flow will achieve. Select one of the templates, if the description seems to fit the flow you want to create. Then you will be taken to the flow builder.

14.2.3.2   Create from My Flows

When you open 'My flows' on the Flow site or select 'See my flows' in the SharePoint Flow dropdown, you will have a choice of creating a flow from scratch or from a template. (The import a flow from another environment only works if you have an additional Plan and several environments.)

When you select to create from a template, you will have the full choice of templates, *see* the image above.

When you select 'Create from blank', you will be asked to select connector for the trigger.

In both cases you will be taken to the flow builder when you have decided the trigger.

14.2.3.3   Create from SharePoint

Click on the Flow button in the command bar, to create a flow directly from a SharePoint list that has the modern interface.

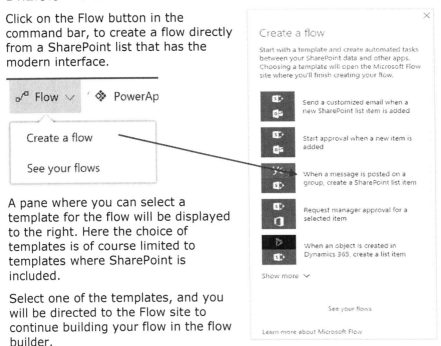

A pane where you can select a template for the flow will be displayed to the right. Here the choice of templates is of course limited to templates where SharePoint is included.

Select one of the templates, and you will be directed to the Flow site to continue building your flow in the flow builder.

14.2.3.4   Renaming

You can rename the titles of the boxes in the flow builder, so that the steps are easy to follow for other people who might edit the flow. Click on the ellipsis at the title and select 'Rename'.

254

You should also give the flow itself a good, descriptive name. Click on the default name to edit it.

14.2.3.5 Finalize the Flow

When you have set the actions and conditions necessary for the flow, click on 'Create Flow' in the top banner to create it.

✓ Create flow

When the flow has been saved, click on 'Done' and the flow will start running when triggered according to the settings of the flow.

▷ Done

14.2.3.6 Edit a Flow

Open 'My flows' on the Flow site or select 'See my flows' in the SharePoint Flow dropdown, and click on the pen icon to edit a flow.

When a flow has been created, a new 'Edit flow' button will be visible to the right above the flow builder. You can also click on that button to edit the flow.

In both cases the flow builder will open in edit mode, and you can make your changes. When you are finished, click on 'Update flow' to the right above the flow builder to save the change.

✓ Update flow

Click on 'Done' in the top banner to finalize the flow.

Microsoft has published lists of references for various connectors at https://docs.microsoft.com/en-us/connectors/. It might be of help when you start creating your own flows.

14.2.4 My Flows

Click on 'My flows' in the Flow top navigation bar to manage your flows. Here you can see a list of all your flows.

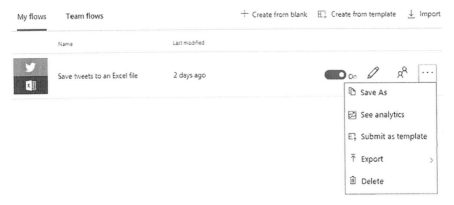

Here you can:

- Turn the flow on or off
- Edit the flow
- Add another owner who also may edit, update and delete this flow
- Create a copy of the flow
- Create a template of the flow
- Export the flow
- Delete the flow

The analytics is a feature that costs extra, and when there is no extra Flow Plan, the link will just give a prompt to upgrade.

14.2.5 Decision Flow that Updates Item and Posts to Facebook

In this flow creation example, I will use a business scenario where a company has three product ranges: Red, Blue and Green. A product manager decides which range each new product should go into.

The company has a SharePoint 'Products' list, where new products are entered as new items. The list has a 'Product Range' column, and the Title column is renamed into 'Product name'. (In the flow it will still be referred to as 'Title'.)

This is what the product decision flow will do: when a new product is added to the 'Products' SharePoint list, the product manager will get an e-mail where he/she can choose range for the new product. When that is done, the new list item will be updated with the chosen range.

There are no conditions for this flow. Instead the flow will always be run when a new item is added to the list.

When the list has been updated with a new product range decision, a status update will be posted to the company page on Facebook. To do that you need to add a connection between your Microsoft Flow account and the Facebook account connected to the company page.

14.2.5.1 Define the Trigger

The first step is to select a template and define where it should be applied.

1. In the 'Products' SharePoint list, click on 'Flow' and select 'Create a Flow'; *refer to* 14.2.3.3 above.

2. Select the template "Send approval email when a new item is added".

3. In this flow, Outlook will perform the action of sending an e-mail to the product manager, and SharePoint will perform the action of updating the 'Products' list, so SharePoint and Outlook are the two flow services involved here.

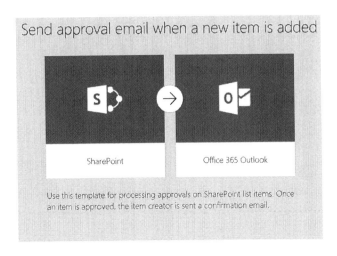

Send approval email when a new item is added

SharePoint

Office 365 Outlook

Use this template for processing approvals on SharePoint list items. Once an item is approved, the item creator is sent a confirmation email.

To use this template:

SharePoint
kate@kalmstrom.com
Switch account

Office 365 Outlook
Sign in required   Sign in

4. (Sign in if needed.)

5. Click on 'Continue' to proceed.

Continue

6. Now you can start building the flow with the parameters you wish to use.

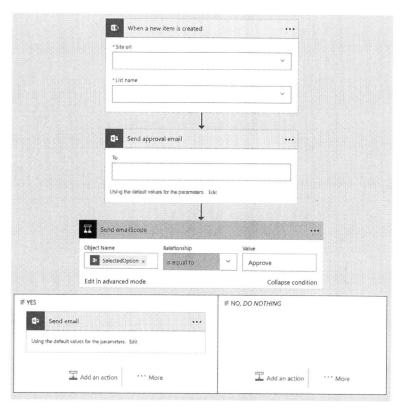

7. In this case, when the flow was created from a SharePoint list, the trigger form 'When a new item is created' has been filled out automatically with the site URL and list name. You can check the values by clicking on 'Edit' to expand the trigger.

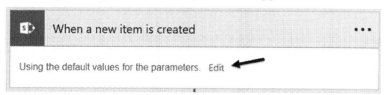

14.2.5.2   Define the 'Send Email' Action

Now we can decide to whom the e-mail should be sent and what it should contain. We will also rename the action so that it will have a more correct name.

1. Enter the e-mail address of the user who will get a message when a product is added to the Projects list.

Using the default values for the parameters   Edit

2. Click on 'Edit' to add new text in the 'Subject' and 'User Options' fields:

   a. To have the product name in the e-mail subject field, type "Product range decision for:" and append 'Title' from the pop-up box with dynamic content to the right.

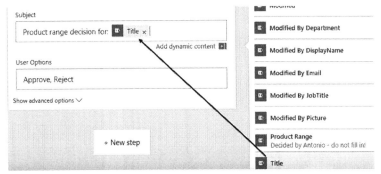

   b. Replace the default user options 'Approve, Reject' with 'Red, Blue, Green', so that any of them can be selected directly in the notification e-mail. Make sure that the options are separated by comma.

3. Click on the ellipsis at the action 'Send approval email' and select 'Rename'. Change the name to "Send decision e-mail".

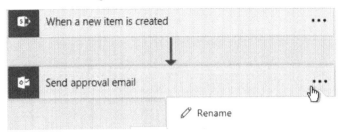

14.2.5.3   Define the 'Update List' Action

In this flow there will be no condition for the e-mail sending, as the e-mail will be sent every time a new item is added to the list. Therefore we can delete the condition step, 'Send emailScope'.

Then we can create the action that will update the Projects list.

1. Select 'New step' and then 'New action' to select the action which will update the SharePoint item.

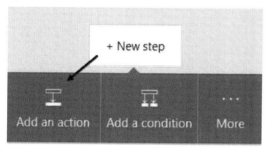

2. As we are going to write back the product range decision to the SharePoint item, select the SharePoint action 'SharePoint – Update item'.

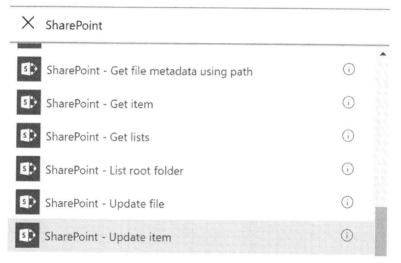

3. Select the website URL in the field 'Site Url' and the 'Products' list under the field 'List name'.

4. Select the field 'ID' from the dynamic content box. This will be the ID from the trigger.

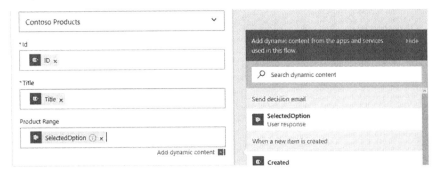

5. Select the field 'Title' from the dynamic content box.

6. In the 'Product range' field, select 'SelectedOption' from the dynamic content pane.

14.2.5.4   Define the 'Post to Facebook' Action

Now we will create an action that will post to the timeline of the company's Facebook profile.

1. Select 'New step' and then 'New action'.

2. Select the action 'Facebook – Post to my timeline'.

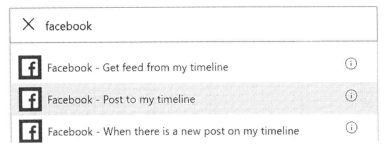

3. Build the Status message:

    a. write "New product launched:"

    b. append the Microsoft parameter 'Title'

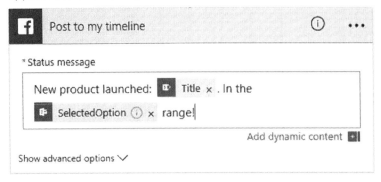

c. write text "In the"

d. append the Microsoft parameter 'SelectedOption'

e. write text 'range!'

Now, look through the flow builder and make sure the step titles and the flow name are descriptive before you finalize the flow.

14.2.5.5   Test the flow

To test the flow:

4. Add a product item in the 'Products' list.

5. Make sure an e-mail is sent.

6. Click on a range in the e-mail.

7. Make sure the SharePoint list is updated.

8. Make sure a status message is posted to Facebook.

Demos:

https://www.kalmstrom.com/Tips/Office-365-Course/First-Microsoft-Flow.htm

https://www.kalmstrom.com/Tips/Office-365-Course/Microsoft-Flow-That-Posts-To-Facebook.htm

14.2.6 Reminder Flow

In this flow example, I will create a flow that sends a reminder e-mail. Such automatic e-mails are good to have when a contract has to be re-negotiated, an important event must be remembered or a subscription should be renewed. These types of reminders can all be automated with a flow similar to this one.

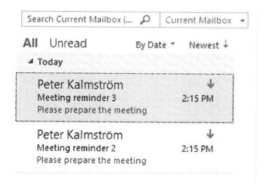

The flow outlined below sends e-mail reminders of events that are created in a SharePoint calendar called "Meetings". It will be created

from a blank template and is connected to a SharePoint calendar and to Office 365 Outlook.

A 'Recurrence' trigger will initiate and repeat the process of sending a reminder at a given time, but at first we will use another trigger that is easier to test: 'SharePoint – When a file is created'. Thus, the flow will first be triggered when a new file is created in a SharePoint library.

The further steps of the flow will be the same as in the final reminder flow. When we have tested the flow with the file creation trigger and seen that it works, we will change the trigger into the recurrence trigger that I actually want to use for this flow.

14.2.6.1 Define the test Trigger

As the calendar list has the classic interface, we cannot start creating the flow from there. Instead, we click on the Flow tile in the Office 365 App Launcher and start with a blank flow in the Flow home page.

1. Select the SharePoint action 'SharePoint – When a file is created'.

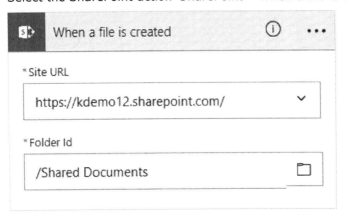

2. Select the SharePoint site URL in the field 'Site URL' and the SharePoint library in the field 'Folder Id'.

14.2.6.2 Define the 'Get items' Action

The first action is to get all the items from the SharePoint calendar.

1. Select 'New step' and then 'New action'.

2. Select the SharePoint action 'SharePoint – Get items'.

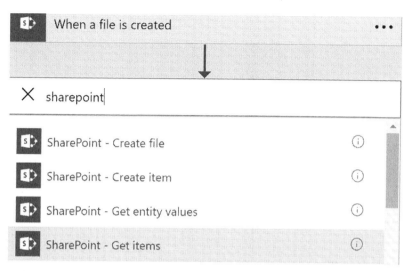

3. Select the website URL in the field 'Site url' and the calendar list in the field 'List name'. (If you cannot find your list in the dropdown, click on 'Enter custom value' at the bottom of the dropdown and enter the list name manually).

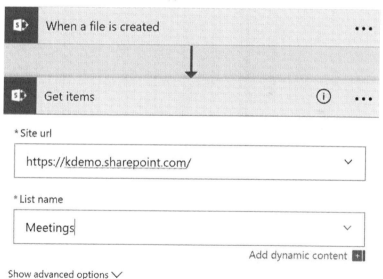

14.2.6.3   Set Conditions

All calendar items were fetched in the action, so now we must set a condition that discerns today's items.

1. Select 'New step' and then 'More' to select `Add an apply to each'. This will run the flow for each item in the list.

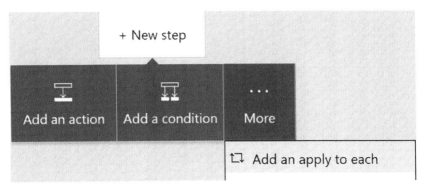

2. Insert the dynamic parameter 'value'.

3. Click on 'Add a condition'.

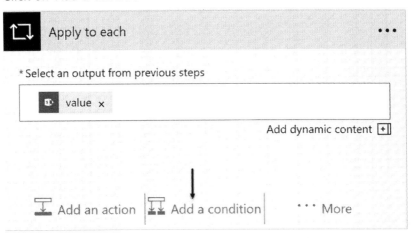

4. Click on 'Edit in advanced mode' and enter the condition '@equals(substring(item()?['EventDate'], 0, 10),utcnow('yyyy-MM-dd'))'.

Condition

Condition

@equals(substring(item()?['EventDate'], 0, 10),utcnow('yyyy-MM-dd'))

Edit in basic mode   Collapse condition

5. Here 'item()' refers to the current item of the list and '['EventDate']' is the column that should be checked. The condition will be true for "Today's Date".

14.2.6.4 Define the 'Sent E-mail' Action

Another action is required to send the e-mail when the condition is true.

1. Click on `Add an action' under `IF YES'.

IF YES, DO NOTHING	IF NO, DO NOTHING
⊥ Add an action ··· More	⊥ Add an action ··· More

2. Select 'Office 365 Outlook - Send an email'.

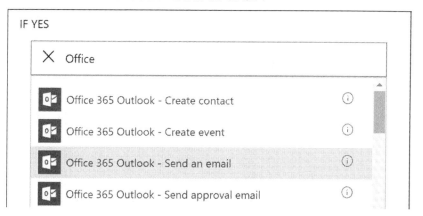

IF YES

✕ Office

Office 365 Outlook - Create contact   ⓘ

Office 365 Outlook - Create event   ⓘ

Office 365 Outlook - Send an email   ⓘ

Office 365 Outlook - Send approval email   ⓘ

3. In the 'To' field, enter the user who will get a reminder e-mail when the condition is true.

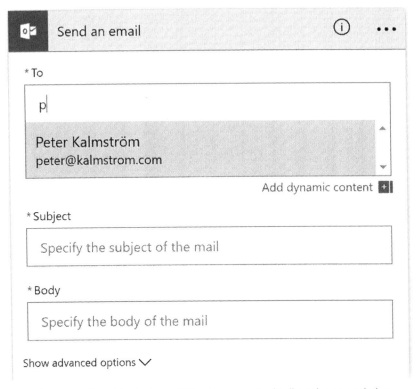

4. For the e-mail subject, type "Meeting reminder" and append the 'Title' of the event.

5. Insert the e-mail body text. You can make it dynamic by using the available parameters.

14.2.6.5   Renaming

Before we finalize the flow we should make the flow and its steps easier to understand.

- Rename 'Apply to each' to "Send e-mails".
- Rename 'Condition' to "Check if item date event is today".
- Rename the Flow to "Send meeting reminders".

14.2.6.6   Test the flow

To test the flow, create a new file in the library specified in the flow trigger. Make sure that an e-mail is sent to the person specified in the flow and that it contains the information specified in step 4 and 5 above.

14.2.6.7 Change to a Reminder Trigger

1. Open the flow builder in edit mode, *refer to* 14.2.3.6 above.

2. Remove the trigger 'SharePoint – When a file is created'.

3. Add a 'Recurrence' trigger.

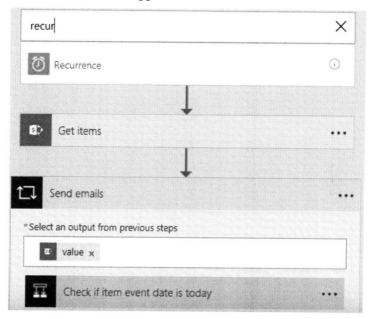

4. Set the time and hour when the flow should be run.

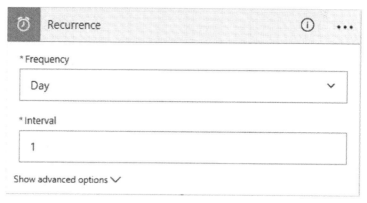

5. Click on 'Update flow' and then 'Done'.

Demo:

https://www.kalmstrom.com/Tips/Office-365-Course/Reminder-Through-Microsoft-Flow.htm

14.2.7 Copy Requested Dropbox files to SharePoint

Sometimes you need to get information from people outside the organization into a SharePoint library, but you don't want to create SharePoint accounts for them. Of course, you can receive files by e-mail and upload them to SharePoint yourself, but that is troublesome. Using a cloud service for document sharing will not burden your mailbox, but it will give the same trouble, and on top of that it will require a login.

A better way is to use a Dropbox "Requested files" folder, and combine it with a flow and a custom library template. "Requested files" folders in Dropbox do not require log in from people who have a link to the folder. A flow can send info from the files in the Dropbox folder into new files in a SharePoint library.

With this method, the process will be automatic, and no login will be required. The solution builds on two preconditions:

- "Requested files" folders in Dropbox do not require log in. A link to the folder is enough.

- When the information uploaded to Dropbox is contained in fields that correspond to SharePoint library columns, a flow can copy field content from "Requested files" into new files in the SharePoint library.

My example uses quotations from restaurants, for a staff party. Such information is not sensitive, so I can use the Dropbox folder without taking risks if the link is shared. The quotation form should be restricted, so that users only can fill out the form and not modify the template.

This is the process:

1. Word files with forms to be filled out are sent to restaurant owners as e-mail attachments. Each e-mail has a link to the "Requested files" folder in Dropbox.

2. Restaurant owners fill out the forms and upload them to the Dropbox "Requested files" folder.

3. A flow copies the information in each filled out Word form to corresponding new files in a SharePoint library, where the suggestions can be seen and rated by the staff.

The library has two custom columns: a "Cost per guest" column and a "Rating" column. Both these columns are shown in the default view. The "Cost per guest" column must have a corresponding field in the Word template, because it needs to be filled out by the people who submit the quotations.

Kick Off Menus

✓	Name ⌄		Cost per guest ⌄	Modified ⌄	Modified By ⌄	Rating (0-5) ⌄
	📄 Kalle Kula - Rest 1.docx	⋯	$99	✱ 2 minutes ago	Peter Kalmström	★★★☆☆ 1
	📄 Stina Stensson - Rest 2.docx		$49	✱ About a minute ago	Peter Kalmström	★★★★★ 1

The creation of a Dropbox "Requested files" folder is out of scope for this book, just as the custom SharePoint library columns and the custom Word form that should be used as a library template. You should have some prior knowledge about all that, to try this solution, but I describe the steps in detail in the Tips article I have linked to below. Here I will concentrate on the flow.

Demo:

https://www.kalmstrom.com/Tips/Office-365-Course/Flow-Dropbox-SharePoint.htm

14.2.7.1   Create the Flow

This flow starts from a blank template. Make sure you have connected your Dropbox account to Flow, *refer to* 14.2.2, before you begin creating the flow.

1. Select the trigger 'Dropbox - when a file is created'.

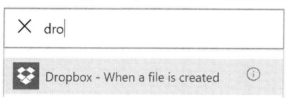

2. Select a Dropbox folder for file requests.

3. Select 'New step' and then 'Add an action' to select the action 'SharePoint – Create file'. This action will create a file in SharePoint based on the uploaded Dropbox file.

4. Select the website URL in the field 'Site Url' and the library path in 'Folder path'.

5. From the dynamic content box, insert the parameters 'File name' in the field 'File name' and 'File content' in the field 'File content'.

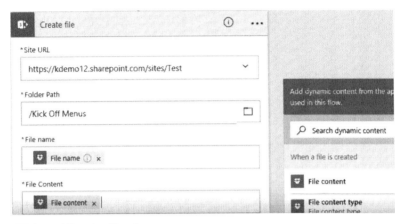

6. Click on 'Create Flow'.

7. Click on 'Done' to finalize the flow.

14.2.7.2 Test the process

1. Send an e-mail to yourself. It should have the Word file attached and a link to the Dropbox "Requested files" folder in the body.

2. Open the document and fill out the form.

3. Click on the link in the e-mail and upload the filled out document to Dropbox.

4. Open the SharePoint document library and refresh the page to see the new document.

5. Make sure that the content is the same as in the file you uploaded to Dropbox.

14.3   POWERAPPS

When an organization uses Office 365 and has its business data in the cloud, staff can reach and work with shared information via the internet using phones, tablets and laptops.

This is convenient and gives freedom to move around, but often the user interface is less satisfying. When you log into a standard Office 365 form or grid from a smart phone with a small touch screen, the interface might be difficult to handle.

This is where the no-code development service PowerApps come in. A powerapp presents data in a more user friendly interface in mobile devices.

With PowerApps, IT professionals can create apps for both mobile and desktop devices and distribute them to users within the organization. Office 365 users can even create their own apps. It is not very difficult to create an auto-generated powerapp, but sometimes it can be tricky to modify it to the optimal design.

PowerApps is much more than another view. From a user perspective, though, a powerapp can be regarded as a touch screen adapted form, where users can view and edit the data that the powerapp is connected to.

Powerapps are not limited to Office 365 but can be connected to other cloud services such as Dynamics CRM, Salesforce, Dropbox and OneDrive and on-premises systems as SharePoint, SQL Server, Oracle databases and SAP. However, the data you want to show in a powerapp must be contained in some kind of grid, like a SharePoint list or an Excel table.

When this is written there are serious limitations, for example that Excel formulas are not supported, but I am sure that Microsoft will enhance PowerApps in the future.

In this section I will show the creation of two powerapps – from an Excel file in OneDrive for Business and from a SharePoint list. Today I find the SharePoint list the most rewarding alternative.

14.3.1 Use a Powerapp

PowerApps has a web player, a mobile player and a Windows desktop player. When you use a powerapp, all changes in the app will be reflected back to the file or list you created the app from, and vice versa.

When you create a powerapp from a SharePoint list, a new view will be added automatically among the list views. That view will have the same name as the app, and it will open in the PowerApps home page.

You can reach your apps at the PowerApps home page. Click on the PowerApps tile in your Office 365 App Launcher, sign in with your Office 365 account and select 'Apps' in the left pane.

You can run, remove, share or edit your apps via the ellipsis on each app icon. Here you can also see details about the app.

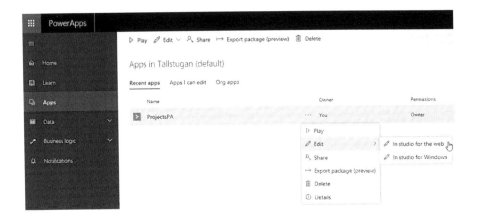

14.3.2 *PowerApps Search*

Powerapps have a search field on top, but currently it is only possible to search text fields. This is a serious limitation, which I hope Microsoft will correct in the future.

14.3.3 *PowerApps Mobile*

When you have PowerApps installed on a smartphone or tablet, you will have the new powerapp among the other apps in your device. You can download PowerApps Mobile from the Windows Store, the App Store or Google Play:

1. Search for PowerApps.

2. Install and open PowerApps. It will now be pinned to your home screen.

3. Sign in with your Office 365 account.

4. Now you will see the apps that you have created and the apps that colleagues have shared with you.

5. Select an app and pin it to your home screen.

PowerApps running on a mobile can take advantage of the location and camera of the device, but you must give your consent to that before you use the app.

14.3.4 *The PowerApps Home Page*

When you click on the PowerApps tile in the Office 365 App Launcher or at office.com, you will be directed to the PowerApps home page at https://web.powerapps.com.

Here is where your apps are stored when you save them to the cloud, and from here you can connect PowerApps to various data sources. The main area has three options for powerapp creation.

- Start by selecting a data source.
- Start with a blank app.
- Start with a template.

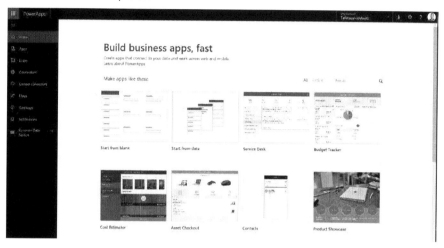

14.3.5 Create an App

Here I will describe the general steps in powerapp creation. There are three ways to start:

- On the PowerApps home page, click on one of the options in the main area to get started, as described above.

- In a SharePoint app with the modern interface, click on the PowerApps button in the command bar. From here you can either start creating a power app from the data in the list or customize the form that is used in the list.

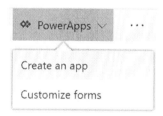

- In PowerApps Studio, *see* below, click on one of the creation options in the main area. You can also click on 'Apps' in the left pane and then 'Create an app'.

 Create an app

14.3.5.1 The PowerApps Studio

Powerapps are edited in the PowerApps Studio for web, at https://create.powerapps.com, or in PowerApps Studio for Windows. The desktop app can be downloaded from Microsoft Store.

Here I will describe the web edition, but the desktop and web PowerApps Studios have a similar interface.

When you go directly to the studio, it will have similar options in the main area as the PowerApps home page.

However, when you start creating your flow, you will be directed to the studio canvas. (If the PowerApps desktop application has already been installed, you will instead be asked to launch the application.) Here you can preview the app that has been created, and you probably want to modify it.

Below I will give two examples on how to create apps in PowerApps, and then I will describe how you can modify them.

14.3.5.2 Create a Powerapp from a OneDrive File

Here I will describe an app creation when we start by selecting the data source OneDrive for Business.

1. Start creating the app from PowerApps home page or studio and select to create from data.

276

2. Click on the Phone layout button below the OneDrive for Business icon. (When this is written, there is no tablet layout for the "Start with your data" option.)

3. Now you are asked to choose a file to create the powerapp from. Even if all folders are displayed, the choice is actually limited to Excel files where the data is formatted as a table.

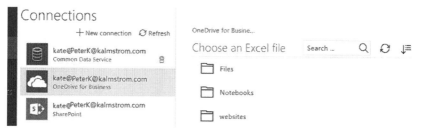

4. Browse to, or search for, a file.

5. Select the table you want to use for the powerapp.

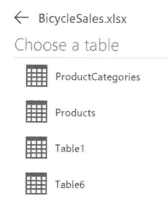

6. Click on the Connect button at the bottom of the screen.

7. Now PowerApps starts to build your new app from the table you specified.

8. The new app will open in Design mode in PowerApps Studio.

It will have a touch friendly design, and you can either use it as it is, *refer to* 14.3.1 or modify it, *refer to* 14.3.6.

14.3.5.3   Create a Powerapp from a SharePoint List

SharePoint lists with the new experience interface has a PowerApps button in the command bar, which makes it very convenient to create apps from them. (The SharePoint command also gives the option to customize the list item form by creating a form app.)

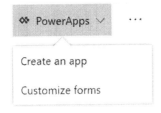

When you select 'Create an app' in the SharePoint list, a pane will open to the right, where you can enter a name for the new app.

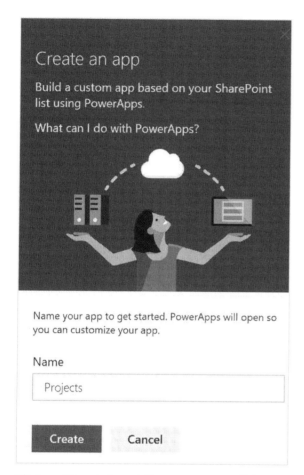

Click on 'Create', and the powerapp will be created from the data in the list where you clicked on the button. It will open in PowerApps Studio.

14.3.5.4   Try a Powerapp

When an app has been created and is displayed in the PowerApps Studio, or when you have made changes to the app, click on the Play button in the right part of the top menu to try the app. Click on the X in the top right corner of the Play screen to go back to the Design canvas.

14.3.5.5   Save a Powerapp

If you are satisfied with the app, open the 'File' tab in the PowerApps studio and save it. You can save the app either to your computer or to the cloud (the PowerApps home page). To share the app, you must save it to the cloud.

The app is by default saved automatically every 2 minutes. You can disable that under File >Account.

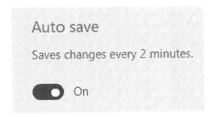

14.3.6 Modify a Powerapp

The design of the automatically created powerapp might not be optimal, but you can make the app more useful and appealing by customizing it. You can for example change which fields are displayed and in which order they are shown. Below are some examples on how you can modify your app.

14.3.6.1 The Design Canvas

The PowerApps Studio Design canvas opens when a new powerapp has been created or when you select to edit an existing powerapp.

The main area, the workspace, displays the app with its different fields or cells, in PowerApps called cards. With the slide control at the bottom of the main area, you can zoom in an out to see the app in the workspace better.

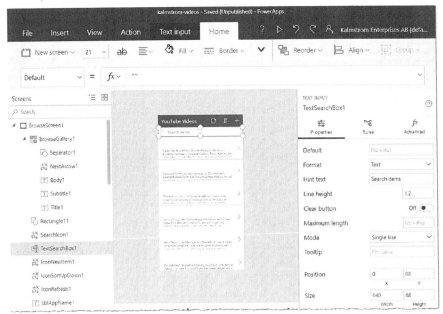

Screens

BrowseScreen1 ···

DetailScreen1 ···

EditScreen1 ···

In the default tree view, *see* the image above, all the controls are listed to the left under the headings BrowseScreen, DesignScreen and EditScreen.

In the thumbnail view, see the image to the left, the left pane shows all the app screens, normally for Browse, Details and Edit. The Details and Edit screens show only one item. Toggle between the two views at the top of the left pane.

The controls in the left pane can be manipulated in various ways via the ellipses. The options vary depending on which control has been selected.

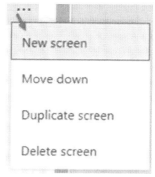

New screen

Move down

Duplicate screen

Delete screen

In both views, click on the card you want to modify to see options in the right pane or above the workspace. In the tree view you can select the card either in the left pane or in the main workspace. In the thumbnail view, select the card in the workspace.

The pane to the right has different content depending on which card is selected. Here you can change which fields will be displayed, in which order they should come, how they should look and much more. The right pane has three tabs, 'Properties' 'Rules' and 'Advanced'.

Above the panes and the workspace, there is a Property dropdown manu, for changes in look and behavior, and a formula bar that shows the value for the selected property. The value can be a number, a string of text or a formula, just like in Excel.

On top of the page there is a ribbon like area with tabs and controls.

281

14.3.6.2 Unlock a Card

You can see that a card is locked for editing, when you set the card and a black locked mark will be visible.

Unlock the card under the 'Advanced' tab in the right pane.

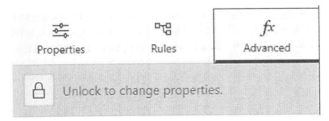

14.3.6.3 Change the Order of Cards

You can easily drag and drop cards to change their order. Select the card, and when the mouse cursor has changed into a cross, drag the card to the place where you want it to be displayed.

14.3.6.4 Change the General Layout

Select 'BrowseGallery' in the left pane tree view (or the Browse tile and then the whole app area) to change the general layout of the app. Click on the 'Layout' link under the 'Properties' tab.

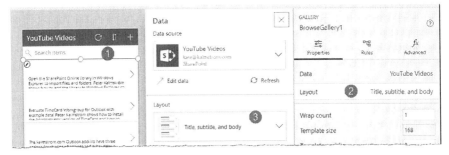

In the new pane that opens, open the Layout dropdown to see the options. When you select 'Blank' you can create the form from scratch.

14.3.6.5 Hide a Field

As the app is meant to be used in mobile devices, you don't want to have too many fields to scroll among. I advise you to hide the card and not delete it, in case you want to use it later.

To hide a field, so that it is not displayed in the app, select the card and set the 'Visible' control under the 'Properties' tab in the right pane to 'Off'.

To show the field again, select the card in the left pane tree view, so that the right pane opens and you can set the control to 'On' again.

14.3.6.6 Change what is Displayed

Maybe the auto-created powerapp does not show the data that is most important to display in an app? In that case, you can change that manually.

Select a control, which might be empty, and change the text in the function field. In the image below, the first data card is empty because it shows a non-existing ComplianceAssetId.

Normally you want the title there, and if you write Title after the dot instead, the card will show the title.

When you have written the first letter, you will have a choice of parameters to add to ThisItem.

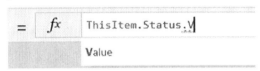

14.3.6.7 Add a Control

If you want to add a extra field on the Browse screen, select the first card in the Browse screen and click on 'Label' under the Insert tab. Change what 'ThisItem' should display, in the way that is described above, and drag the new field to the place where you want it to be displayed in the cards on the Browse screen.

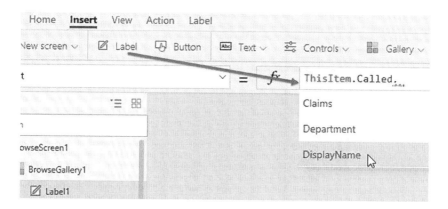

14.3.6.8 Change the Search Parameter

Select the BrowseGallery to see how the auto-generated powerapp searches among data. In the image below, the app searches on ComplianceAssetId, but most often you want the title to be searched.

The formula below is the same as in the image above, except that it has been changed so that the search is performed on the title field:

SortByColumns(Filter(Projects, StartsWith(Title, TextSearchBox1.Text)), "Title", If(SortDescending1, Descending, Ascending))

14.3.6.9 Change Text Color for a Specified Field Value

You can add conditional formatting to text. To change the text color when a field has a specific value, select the card where you want to add the conditional formatting.

Then select the property you want to change in the top left dropdown. In the image below, the property 'Color' has been selected, and the function field shows the default RGBA color. You can however add a condition to it.

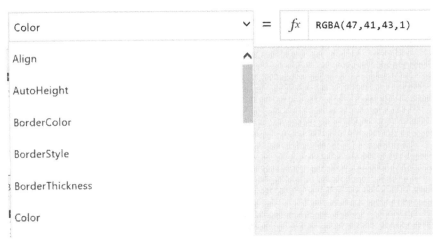

For exampe, 'If(ThisItem.Status.Value = "In Progress",Green,RGBA(47,41,43,1))' will make the text in the Status field green when its value is 'In Progress'.

14.3.7 Share a Powerapp

To share a powerapp, you need to first save it manually to the cloud and then publish it. In PowerApps Studio, open the File tab and click on first 'Save' and then 'Publish'.

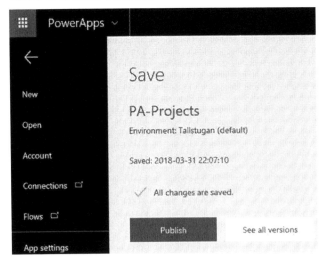

Now the powerapp will be available for sharing, and instead of the 'Publish' button there is a 'Share this app' button. You can also select 'Share' in the left pane.

The Share command will direct you to the PowerApps home page at https://web.powerapps.com.

If you instead start from the home page, you can click on 'Apps' in the left pane to open your apps, and then click on 'Share' under the ellipsis of the app you want to share.

Now you can start writing the names or e-mail addresses of the people or groups that you want to share your app with, and select among the suggestions that will come up.

You can also share your app with the whole organization. It is however only possible to share powerapps with users of the same Office 365 tenant.

You can decide if an e-mail with a link to the new app should be sent to people with whom you have shared the powerapp.

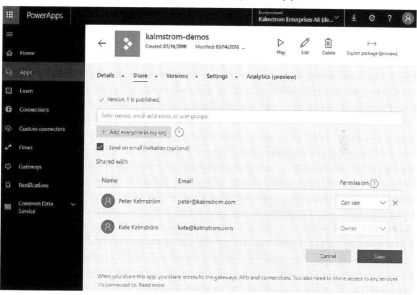

You can also set permissions on the app for the people or groups you share it with. "Can use" gives permission to run the app but not share it, while "Can edit" users can run and customize the app and share it to other users. If you share with the whole organization, you can only give "Can use" permission.

For some data sources, read permissions are given automatically when an app is shared. In other cases, the app creator must share the data source, or the user must take steps to connect to the data source.

14.3.7.1 Publish changes

When you want to propagate your changes to a shared app, you must first publish it with the 'Publish' button under the 'Files' tab.

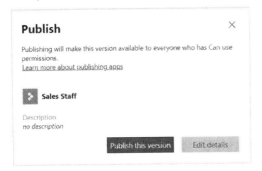

Be aware that any changes you make to a shared app will flow through to the people you shared it with as soon as you have published your changes. This is good when you improve the app, but if you remove or significantly change features, it may have a negative impact on other users.

Demos:

https://www.kalmstrom.com/Tips/Office-365-Course/First-Powerapp.htm

https://www.kalmstrom.com/Tips/Office-365-Course/Phone-Powerapp.htm

14.4 SUMMARY

In this chapter we have looked at Flows and PowerApps, two Microsoft services that have some common features even if they are intended for different purposes.

Flow is an automation tool and Microsoft's future replacement for SharePoint workflows in Office 365. I have described the basics in flow creation and management and also given a few example flows that can be useful within an organization.

PowerApps is a fairly new service that makes it possible to create apps that show list or grid data in a mobile and touch friendly interface.

I have shown some examples on what you can do, and I hope my descriptions will act as a starting point for your own app creation. I have also explained how to share a powerapp and what to think about when you share powerapps.

15 POWER BI

BI means Business Intelligence, and Power BI is a
business analytics service that lets you create
visualizations of data from unrelated sources in a way
that reminds of the Excel pivot table.

A Power BI report is however much more user friendly and intuitive and
can be used more extensively. The Power BI reports are business apps
that run in a browser or on a phone or tablet.

In Business Intelligence there are two distinct ways of building reports.
One method is that the company launches a major effort to consolidate
all data from different sources into a data warehouse. This is usually a
very big and difficult project and will not be covered in this book.

The other type of Business Intelligence "project" is a user with some
data in Excel or text files which he/she wishes to explore or build reports
on. This second type of Business Intelligence project is usually
categorized as Self-service BI. Microsoft Power BI supports both these
types of Business Intelligence.

Power BI is not displayed among the Office 365 tiles in the App Launcher
until the user has signed up for the service, and in most organizations
only a few Office 365 users will create Power BI reports. Power BI gives
huge possibilities when it comes to visualizing data from different
sources, a so called dataset, but it is a complex application that takes
some time to learn. It helps if you are used to working with Excel and
databases, of course. Here I will just give an overview of the basics.

The majority of users will study and interact with Power BI reports when
these are added to other sites or apps, and for that you don't need to
sign up. Users can also view and interact with Power BI reports in the
Power BI mobile apps. Windows Phone, Android and iOS are supported.

Power BI reports are often created in the Power BI desktop app and then
published to the Power BI web service, where you create new
visualizations or build dashboards to share with colleagues. You can also
start in the web service directly and create everything there, but the
desktop app gives more design options.

15.1 PRO AND PREMIUM

Power BI comes in three editions, and only the most limited one, which I
describe here, is free. If you want to have more advanced features, you
must add a Pro or Premium subscription.

However, just as in the case of Flow and PowerApps, Microsoft is using
the same interface for the free edition and the paid ones and gives an
upgrade prompt when you try to use paid features with the free edition.

All images below are taken from a standard Enterprise subscription with the free Power BI. This means that some of the icons and links you see on the images do not work, but everything I describe is of course included in the free edition.

15.2 SIGN UP FOR POWER BI

For users with an Office 365 Enterprise subscription, it is free and easy to sign up for Power BI. Go to https://powerbi.microsoft.com/ and click on the 'START FREE' button.

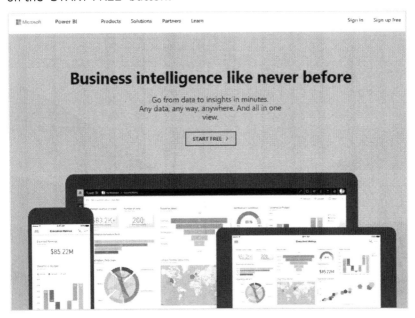

Now you will have two options, download the desktop edition of Power BI or use the web service edition. (There is also an option for on-premises deployment, but it is not interesting here.)

Start sharing your data visualizations and insights

POWER BI	POWER BI REPORT SERVER
Cloud collaboration and sharing	On-premises report deployment
Use Power BI Pro to share and distribute reports with others, without any complicated setup. Get started now with a free 60-day trial of Power BI Pro.	Deploy and distribute interactive Power BI reports—and traditional paginated reports—within the boundaries of your organization's firewall.

15.2.1 Power BI Service

When you select to use the Power BI web service, you are asked to sign in with your Office 365 account, and after that you will have an option to send invitations to colleagues.

When the setup has finished, you can see the Power BI tile among the other Office 365 tiles, and you can start using the service.

15.2.2 Power BI Desktop

If you select to start with the web service, you can always get both desktop and mobile editions later, from the right navigation bar in the web service or under 'Products' in the Power BI "Get started" page.

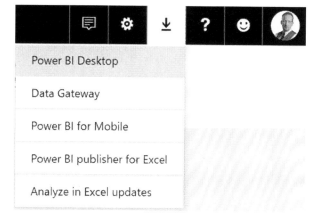

Power BI Desktop is actually only a design tool for Power BI reports. It has a ribbon with many options to enhance the report. Some of these options are available in the service too, but not all of them.

If you select to create the report in the desktop edition, you must still publish it to the service before you can share anything more than the report file.

15.3 Reports and Dashboards

A Power BI dashboard is a canvas page in Power BI Service that contains a number of tiles and widgets. Each tile displays a single visualization, also called visual, that was created from a dataset and pinned to the dashboard. A dashboard can display such visuals from several different datasets.

A Power BI report is one or more pages of visuals (charts, graphs and images) of data from one single dataset. A Power BI report can be created in either Power BI Service or Power BI Desktop.

15.4 Get a Dataset

The collection of data that Power BI uses to create visuals is called a dataset. The dataset provides the data, metrics, and information that's displayed in your Power BI dashboard.

You can have a very simple dataset based on a single table from an Excel workbook. A dataset can also consist of a combination of data from several different sources, for example from an Access or SQL database, from Azure or Oracle and/or from services like Facebook and Salesforce. Power BI has built-in data connectors that let you connect to the data, filter it if necessary and bring it into your dataset.

To get data for your Power BI report you can use content packs from outside services, upload your own data or connect to a database. The image below comes from the web service. The desktop edition instead has a ribbon button that opens a dropdown with similar options.

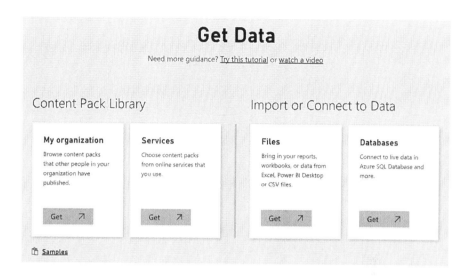

15.4.1 Get Data from File

When you have made your selection you can specify which kind of data source you want to use. The image below shows the choices when 'Files' has been selected in the 'Get Data' page.

OneDrive for Business and SharePoint are the recommended sources for the 'Files' option, as they are both in the cloud. If any changes are found in the file, your dataset, reports, and dashboards are automatically updated in Power BI. The last of the tiles in the image below links to a detailed explanation about file import.

When you select to use a SharePoint file, you can either enter a site URL or click on Connect to have a choice of available apps and then files.

Enter Site URL to Connect to

Sharepoint site URL (Example: https://contoso.sharepoint.com/teams/sales)

ⓘ Do not have the URL handy? You can click Connect to see the content available to you at the root level.

Connect   Cancel

If you instead use OneDrive for Business, you will see available folder and files at once.

When a file has been selected you can either import or connect it to Power BI. The dataset will be added to Power BI in a new dashboard, where you can create visualizations by asking questions about the data, *refer to* 15.5.2, or by using the report editor.

The desktop edition shows the dataset in a report editor.

15.5 VISUALS

When you have your dataset, you can start creating visuals of different portions of the data. These visualizations can be in different forms, for example charts, graphs or color-coded maps. A collection of visuals built on the same dataset constitutes a Power BI report.

15.5.1 Insights

When you start working on the dashboard, you will be asked if you want to use Insights. This means that Power BI quickly searches different subsets of your dataset while applying a set of sophisticated algorithms to discover potentially-interesting insights.

NAME	ACTIONS	OWNER
☆ BicycleSales ✳		Kate Kalmström

You can also always reach the Insights feature from My Workspace >Reports (above) and from the ellipsis at the top right corner of the tiles on the dashboard (below).

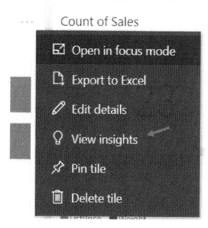

Count of Sales

- ⊡ Open in focus mode
- ⧉ Export to Excel
- ✎ Edit details
- ◯ View insights
- ⚲ Pin tile
- 🗑 Delete tile

Many of these auto-generated visuals will not be interesting to you, but when you find one that you want to include in your report you can just pin it to the dashboard – or to another dashboard. *Refer* to 15.5.3 below.

15.5.2 Q&A

The easiest way to create a visual is actually to ask questions on your data in the Power BI web service. You can write the question in natural language, and the service will create visuals based on your question. By clicking on the underlined words in your question, you can select new options and refine or expand the visualization and find new results.

In the image below the question is "How many bikes were sold in 2015 grouped by color?" and the words "bikes", "2015" and "color" are underlined. This means that you can click on them and get other parameters for products, years or grouped by.

How many bikes were sold in 2015 grouped by color?

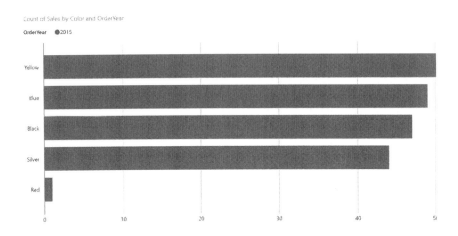

15.5.3 Pin Visual to Dashboard

When you have created a visual that you like in the service, you can click on 'Pin visual' in the top right corner of the tile and pin it to a dashboard. The visual will then be placed in a tile on the workspace of the dashboard you select, and there you can work more with it and adapt it to other visuals that are placed there.

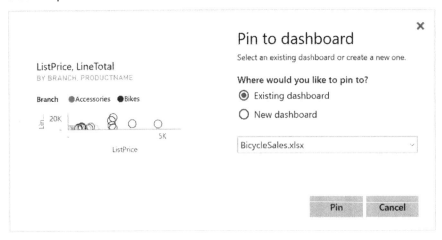

15.5.4 Phone View

When you have pinned a visual, you will be asked to optimize the report for a mobile device. If you do that, a phone view of the report will open in the dashboard, and you can edit it – for example hide some visuals.

You can always reach the phone view via the dropdown in the top right corner of the workspace.

15.5.5 The Report Editor

Instead of asking questions you can play around with your data and create your own visualizations in the report editor. In the service, click on the dataset in the dashboard to reach the workspace where you create visualizations.

In the desktop edition the dataset is placed in the report editor from the beginning, and you can always reach it by selecting the chart icon in the top left corner under the ribbon.

The report editor has a left pane with all the columns from the dataset and various visualization and filter options. Columns marked with Σ are in number format.

Check a column, or drag it on to the canvas. Then you can select chart styles and continue to add more columns, filters, report levels and values.

Each visual is contained in a rectangular box called a tile, and you can drag these tiles as you wish to change their size and position.

You can drag more columns into the first tile, or put the tiles side by side. They will still be connected, so that if you for example check a box in a slicer in one tile, the other tiles will be updated. In the image below, both charts are updated when you select a branch in the slicer.

Demo:

http://www.kalmstrom.com/Tips/Office-365-Course/Power-BI-Intro.htm

15.6   SHARE

When you have created a collection of visuals that you want to share with others, you can do that in several ways. You can save your desktop work in Power BI Desktop file format, with the .pbix extension, and such files can be shared like any other file.

When you upload Power BI Desktop files to the Power BI Service, you will have more options to share them.

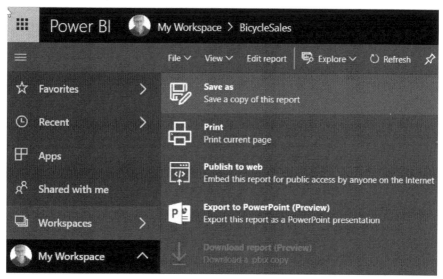

The Power BI 'Publish to web' feature gives an embed code that you can copy and paste into a SharePoint page or another web page. This method works well when you want to show public data, but it is not secure. It gives a link that does not require a login, so anyone who has the embed link can access the report in Power BI.

For data that should be kept secure, I recommend you to insert a screenshot of the report in the web page and link it to Power BI. If you copy the URL from the address field in the report, users will be asked to log in when they click on the linked screenshot.

When you add a Power BI web part to a modern SharePoint page, you should also use the report address, *refer to* 6.3.2.2.

The option 'Export to PowerPoint' is suitable for reports with many pages, as each page will be transferred to a slide, but there is no possibility for viewers to interact with or manipulate the data.

Demo:

https://kalmstrom.com/Tips/Office-365-Course/Power-BI-Embed.htm

15.7 SUMMARY

A full description on all the possibilities given by Power BI is out of scope for this book, but in this chapter I have given an introduction and mentioned the most important terms and features. When you now have learned the basics and know what things are called, it will be easier to find more information on the internet and in other books.

16   SWAY

Sway is a presentation app where users work on a web-based canvas. It is possible to insert images, text, documents, videos, charts and maps from many different sources into the presentation – which is called a "sway". Sway may of course also be used for reports, newsletters, personal stories, tutorials and so on.

Everyone with a Microsoft account can use Sway for free, but Office 365 subscribers can take advantage of considerably higher content limits per sway.

Sways automatically adapt to devices with different screen sizes, and it is easy to build nice looking presentations with Sway. The users add content and select from various options how it should be presented, and the app suggests presentation design and layout from that input. You can even enter a topic and have an auto-generated sway about that topic!

The Sway home page shows sways created by you, templates for new sways and sways to get inspiration from.

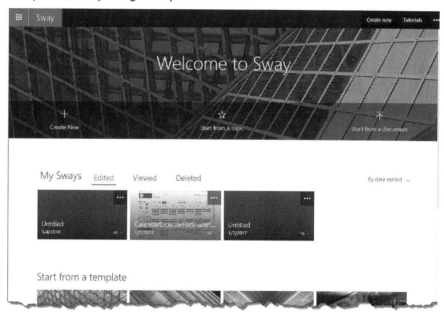

Sway and PowerPoint share a similar goal: to present information in a compelling, visual way, often as a help to a speaker. Technically they are very different. From a feature standpoint Sway makes it easier for users to create stunning visual effects, while PowerPoint gives you more control over the details.

You don't have full control when you use Sway, even if the options are many, and currently you have to accept a 'Made with Sway' message at the end of each sway you create.

Another drawback is that sways are stored in Azure in Microsoft's data centers, not in OneDrive or SharePoint, and there is no possibility to use the sway off-line or save it "as". There is a Sway desktop app, but even if you use it you have to go online to view or edit sways.

16.1 SWAY ADMIN SETTINGS

By default, Sway is enabled for all users in the tenant and external sharing is allowed, but administrators can control that in the Office 365 Admin center >Settings >Services & add-ins >Sway.

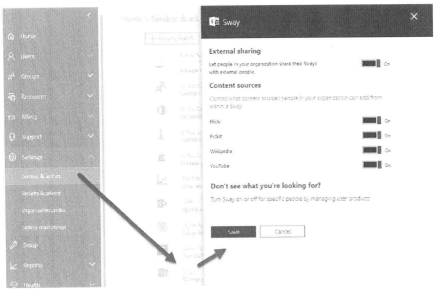

In the right pane that opens, you can turn off external sharing and limit from where users can add content to sways they create. The image above shows the default settings, which are all 'On'.

You can also turn Sway off for specific users, *refer to* 3.1.2.1.2.

16.2 CREATE A SWAY

A new sway can be created in four ways:

- Upload a document and let Sway create a sway from it.

- Enter a topic in a search box. If Sway finds any hits, content is auto-generated.

- Start with a template.

- Start from scratch with a new sway.

When you use the two first options you have to modify the automatically generated sway, and the steps to do that are the same as when you create a sway from scratch. When you create a sway from a template, you will get hints in the template on how you can personalize it.

The Sway user interface and the way you work with it reminds of modern SharePoint page, and however you choose to start a new sway, it is easy to create and edit it.

Here I will create a sway from scratch, by clicking on the 'Create New' button or the 'Create new' link on the Sway home page.

16.2.1 Storyline Tab

Cards are the Sway building blocks, and when you create a sway you use the cards to insert and arrange the content. Each card represents one piece of content. You can drag and drop the cards, to change their order.

The cards are arranged in a storyline, and you create a sway by adding content cards to that storyline. The Storyline Tab is default when you start creating a new sway.

Below is the first card in the storyline when a sway is created from scratch. Here you can type a title or paste a link and add a background image. Click on 'Emphasize' to tell Sway what is most important or add italic to text by clicking on 'Accent'.

Click on the plus sign to have more options.

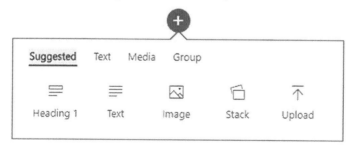

303

In the image below I have Emphasized "Sweden", added Accent to 'Spring' and inserted a link with the caption "from Swedish grammar".

I have also added a background image and clicked on 'Focus Points' to tell Sway what is important in the image. In this case I checked the box 'The entire image is important'.

Sway picks the best layout depending on your device and style.

When the first card is finished, I can click on the plus sign below it to have new options for the next card.

When you select to add an image or video, an insert pane will open to the right. You can also click on the 'Insert' button to open it. Here you will have many suggestions on media to use. I recommend that you keep the 'Creative Commons Only' box checked, so that you don't use copyright protected work by mistake.

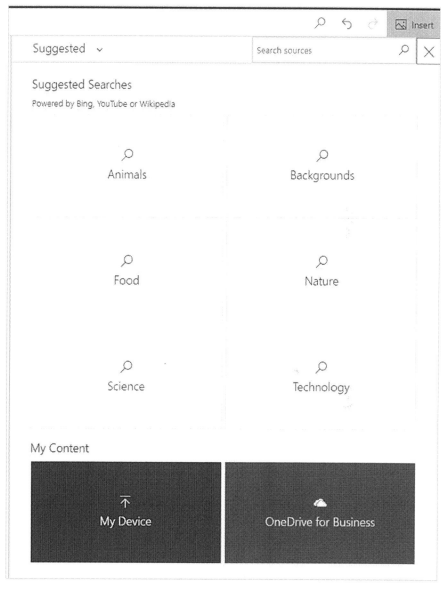

You may of course also upload your own media to Sway.

The little checkbox at the bottom right of the card is for selection. Check it when you want to include the card in your sway. Uncheck it again to exclude the card without removing it.

16.2.2 Play

Above the storyline, to the right, there is a Play and a Share button.

Click on 'Play' to see how the sway will look when finished.

In the Play mode, the top right buttons are different. The icons are back to editing, autoplay settings and share. (You will find more settings options when you go back to edit mode and click on the ellipsis there.)

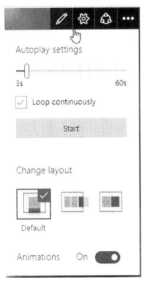

16.2.3 Design Tab

The Design tab shows a similar main area as the Play mode, but it has a 'Styles' command to the right which opens a pand with many design options. Via the 'Customize' button you can also create your own design.

There are three layout options: vertical (default) and horizontal scroll and slides layout.

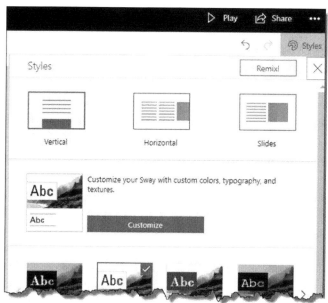

When you click on the Remix button, Sway will suggest combinations of the design and navigation choices you have made for your sway.

The arrows for undo/redo are the same as in the Office applications.

16.2.4 Share

The Share command lets you decide how your sway should be shared. By default, sways are shared within the tenant, but you can also share with specific people or with anyone.

You can allow people to edit and share the sway, and for better security you can require a password to view or edit the sway. There are also options for an embed code and a visual link.

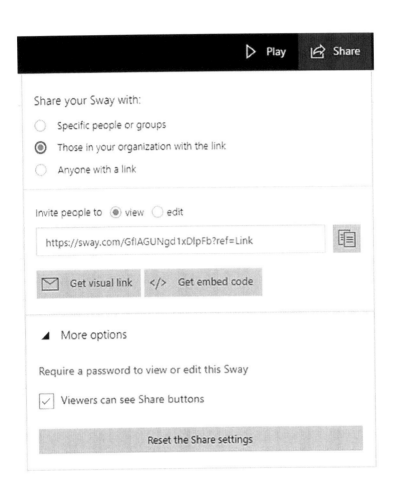

16.2.5 More options

Under the ellipsis you can find various links. The Storyline tab gives the most options.

'Print' and 'Export' are nearly the same, because when you choose 'Print' a printable PDF file will be created from the sway. The 'Export' link also gives the option to save the sway as a Word file.

The settings give more options than the Autoplay options under the Play mode settings gear. Maybe you have no objections to allowing viewers to duplicate or change the layout of your sway, but you should be aware that you permit this if you don't uncheck the boxes under View settings.

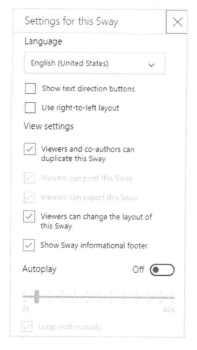

With the Accessibility Checker and Accessibility View you can improve accessibility, for example by adding alternative texts to images and good display texts to links.

Demo:

https://www.kalmstrom.com/Tips/Office-365-Course/Sway.htm

16.3   SUMMARY

With Sway, Microsoft has really made an effort to explain to users how to manage Sway, so after my introduction I hope you have had the overview that is necessary to start playing with the app and creating your own sways.

I also hope you are now aware that Sway's easiness has a price. Therefore Sway presentations are probably not the best option at all times, even if the sways look good and can be created quickly.

17 FORMS

When users click on the Forms tile in the Office 365 App Launcher or at office.com, they will be directed to http://forms.microsoft.com.

Forms is a new service that has been available for Office 365 educational subscriptions for some time but now has been released in Preview to commercial subscriptions as well.

This means that commercial subscribers currently get the same features and service quality as Office 365 education subscribers. Microsoft will tailor the experience for more commercial scenarios, so Business and Enterprise subscriptions will see changes in Forms in the near future.

With Forms, you can create surveys, quizzes, and polls and easily see the results as they come in. People can respond using a web browser or mobile device.

To evaluate the responses, you can use the built-in analytics or export the data to Excel for additional analysis.

17.1 USER INTERFACE

The user interface of the Forms home page is very simple. To the left there are tabs for forms and quizzes created by you (default) and shared with you. The third tab is for forms and quizzes created in Teams or SharePoint. They will show up here automatically.

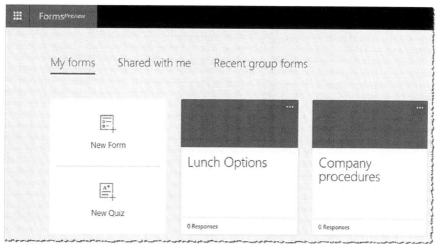

Under the 'My forms' tab there are buttons for form and quiz creation. When you click on one of them, a blank form with two tabs will open. Add your questions under the 'Questions' tab and see the answers under the 'Responses' tab.

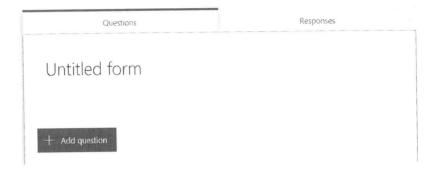

17.2 ADMIN SETTINGS

In the Office 365 Admin center >Settings >Services & add-ins >Microsoft Forms, administrators can turn off the default possibility to share forms and results with users outside the organization.

When a setting is turned off, only people within organization will have access to that option, and only when they are signed in.

The image below shows the default settings, where everything is allowed.

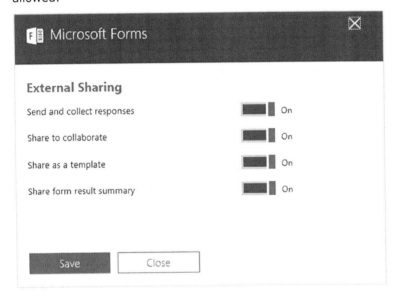

17.3 CREATE A FORM

The Form option is meant for polls and surveys, where you want to know people's opinion about things. You can also use a form when you want to mesaure knowledge but not show the correct answers or give points for them.

When you click on the 'Add question' button in the 'New Form' dialog, you will have several options on how people should answer your questions.

For the 'Text' option, the answers must be written in, but you can restrict them to be a number and even limit the number span.

The 'Likert' option under the ellipsis is easy to answer, because here the respondents just have to rate how much they think a statement is right or wrong.

Also the 'Rating' and the default 'Choice' are easy for respondents to fill out, as they only have to select a radio button.

When the first question has been finished, click on 'Add question' again to continue with the next one.

The form is saved automatically, so you can just click on 'Forms Preview' in the left Office 365 navigation bar to go back to the start page.

17.3.1 Edit

Click on a question to edit it. In the top right corner of each question in edit mode, you can find icons for copying and deleting the question and for moving the question up and down in the form.

17.4 CREATE A QUIZ

Use the quiz option when you want to measure knowledge and the answers are right or wrong. Quizes give some options to show correct answers, give points for them and even point respondents in the right direction towards a correct answer.

All question alternatives in a quiz have a Points field, where you can give the weight of the question.

Some of the question types also have other options:

313

- If you create a Choice question, you will have the option to give a message when an answer is selected and to mark one of the answers as the correct one.

- The Text option lets you enter the correct answer(s), to be shown to the respondent.

The rest of the question options do not give more options than in the form, except the weight points.

17.5   BRANCHING AND SETTINGS

When a form or quiz is open, you can find links to branching and settings under the ellipsis in the top right corner. The branching and settings options are the same for forms and quizzes.

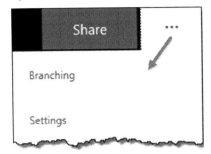

17.5.1 Branching

When you click on 'Branching' all choice questions will have an option to continue in a specific way: to the next question, to another question or to the end of the form.

With branching you can follow up with questions that only apply for certain answers and/or let respondents skip questions that are not relevant to them.

17.5.2 Settings

The image below shows the default settings. The non-default option include a start and end date for the form or quiz and an e-mail notification of each response. You can also set the questions to be shown in random order for each respondent.

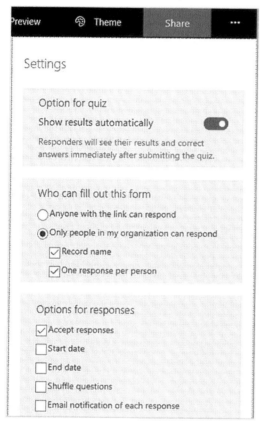

17.6 SHARE

A form or quiz can be shared in several ways. To send it to the respondents, select one of the four options and copy the link/embed code if needed.

These are the options:

- Copy a link and paste it in a shared area, for example a chat.

- Download a QR-code (selected option in the image below) and paste it where your intended audience can scan it, for example with a mobile device.

- Copy the embed code and embed the form or quiz into a blog, a SharePoint page or other web page.

- Send a link in an e-mail by selecting the fourth option. This opens an e-mail with the link and some explaning (editable) text. The first time you use this option, you must specify from what e-mail account the e-mail should be sent.

The respondent setting on top of the Share pane synchronizes with the option selected in the settings.

In the Share pane you can also share the form or quiz to people who are not supposed to answer it:

- Get a template link. All receivers of this link can use our form or quiz as a template. Responses are not included.

- Get a collaboration link. Receivers of this link can work on the form or quiz, for example add or remove questions, see the responses and share the form or quiz with others. By default, anyone with the link can collaborate, but you can select to restrict the permission to people within the tenant.

Create your group forms in Teams or SharePoint, and we'll put them here.

17.6.1 Check Results

To see the answers as they come in, open the 'Responses' tab in your form or quiz and see statistics. For more elaborate analysis you can open the results in Excel directly from the 'Responses' tab.

17.6.1.1 Response limit

You can receive up to 5000 responses. If you need more, export the existing responses to Excel and then clear them from the form or quiz 'Responses' tab. Once the tab is cleared, you can receive more responses.

Demo:

https://www.kalmstrom.com/Tips/Office-365-Course/Forms.htm

17.7 SUMMARY

Office 365 offers other survey options, like the SharePoint survey and the Excel survey, but Forms is easy to use, and the resulting questionnaires adapt well to different screen sizes.

In this last chapter we have seen how forms and quizzes can be created and shared. You should also know about branching and settings and understand how to analyze the results when the answers come in.

18   ABOUT THE AUTHOR

Peter Kalmstrom is the CEO and Systems Designer of the Swedish family business Kalmstrom Enterprises AB, well known for the software brand *kalmstrom.com Business Solutions*. Peter has 19 Microsoft certifications, among them several for SharePoint, and he is a certified Microsoft Trainer.

Peter begun developing his kalmstrom.com products around the turn of the millennium, but for a period of five years, after he had created *Skype for Outlook*, he also worked as a Skype product manager. In 2010 he left Skype, and since then he has been concentrating on his own company and on lecturing on advanced IT courses.

Peter has published three more books, *SharePoint Online from Scratch*, *SharePoint Online Exercises* and *Excel 2016 from Scratch*. All are sold worldwide via Amazon.

As a preparation for lectures and books, Peter has created various video demonstrations, which are available on YouTube and at https://www.kalmstrom.com/Tips.

Peter divides his time between Sweden and Spain. He has three children, and apart from his keen interest in development and new technologies, he likes to sing and act. Peter is also a dedicated vegan and animal rights activist.

19 INDEX